OTHER BOOKS BY MARGARET BOYLES

The Margaret Boyles Book of Crewel Embroidery
The Margaret Boyles Book of Needle Art
The Margaret Boyles Bargello Workbook
American Indian Needlepoint Workbook
Bargello: An Explosion in Color
Needlepoint Stitchery

Margaret Boyles'

NEEDLEWORK GIFTS

for Special Occasions

SIMON AND SCHUSTER   NEW YORK

For Justin, my blue-eyed boy

10 9 8 7 6 5 4 3 2 1

Library of Congress Cataloging in Publication Data

Boyles, Margaret.
   Margaret Boyles' Needlework gifts, for special
occasions.

   1. Needlework.   I. Title.   II. Title: Needlework
gifts for special occasions.
TT750.B74   746.44   81-1311
                            AACR2
ISBN 0-671-25322-0

Contents

Woolen Mufflers and Needlepoint Pillows

Red woolen mufflers, lovingly knit black stockings, toasty warm handmade mittens, soft quilts made from myriad scraps of fabric—all conjure up happy memories of stories we read as children about pioneer families toiling to tame the wilderness and make a new life. Always, as the winter snows piled high, the household stores grew small and anxious parents fretted that there would be no gifts to cheer little ones on Christmas morning. It was a heartbreaking prospect, but somehow the miracle always occurred and a tree, brightly wrapped packages, and the ingredients for a feast livened the holiday. When the packages were opened, the muffler was always red and woolly and indescribably warm, and the stockings were utilitarian black and scratchy but knit with such love that they were absolutely beautiful.

It is probably nostalgic memories of those stories combined with some very real recollections of those warm and homely Christmases that stir in all of us real pleasure in making, giving and receiving handmade gifts. The love perceived in these transcends the size of the present and bestows upon it importance rarely achieved by a purchased offering no matter what its cost.

There is no doubt about it, we all love handmade gifts. We like to make them and love to receive them. When the idea for a book of embroidered gifts was advanced, my first image was a combination of holidays and special occasions, designed greeting-card style, with an especially conceived project to commemorate each occasion. There would be an amusing sampler of New Year's resolutions, a lacy heart-shaped pillow for a Valentine, a golden wedding bell design for a fiftieth wedding anniversary, a huge needlepoint stocking for a baby's first Christmas. Mother's Day, Father's Day, graduation, Hanukkah and birthdays would be represented.

It was an intriguing idea, but one quickly discarded as too contrived, too trite. Real people give meaningful presents especially when they are going to spend countless hours making them. A Mother's Day pillow emblazoned *For Mom* may be loved and appreciated, but it will soon disappear from its place of honor in the living room. A pretty pillow in good taste, style, and color to complement the room will be used and loved for years—and Mom will never need be reminded who made it or when!

And so the book is filled with the things you like to make and give—pretty pillows, pictures, cross-stitch samplers, linens, accessories, Christmas ornaments—for birthdays, weddings, anniversaries, thank-you's, graduations, housewarmings, and on down the long list of occasions and celebrations we love to brighten with gifts.

An embroidered gift is really something special—you put something of yourself into every stitch—and it can be made even more meaningful if you initial and date it. Mom won't need the reminder, but she will be pleased with this final flourish. On a sampler, do this in the lower border; a pillow can be personalized on either the front or back; use the entire back of a pincushion for your message; sign the wrong side of a place mat hem; put a note on the back of a framed picture; leave one more little part of yourself for the recipient to enjoy in the years to come.

The initials and date can be very inconspicuous—pale beige yarn on white, a shade lighter or darker than the background color in most cases. Or you can be as gay as sunshine and make your signature bright and a part of the design itself.

If you do a lot of needlepoint, develop a little design combining your initials and use it consistently on all your work. It does not have to be elaborate or fancy. Plot it out on graph paper—you can use all three initials, the first and last, or only the last. You might like the look of just your last initial with a square, diamond, or rectangular outline; perhaps all three letters with the last worked larger and in the center. This arrangement can be worked into a diamond shape which is very pretty.

For a crewel gift nothing could be more meaningful than your own signature worked in Back or Outline Stitch. Make a little transfer pattern, then embroider.

Some ideas used for the gifts in this book: An envelope glued to the back of the Pennsylvania Dutch Wedding Sampler contains a letter with a brief history of the original Pennsylvania frakturs and a photograph of the one from which the design was adapted (it records the baptism of the bride's great-great-great grandmother). The piece itself is initialed and dated under the mat. The carnation pillow has the recipient's and the maker's names worked right into the two partial flowers at the bottom. The Pastel Bargello Pincushion says *Happy Birthday, Jane!*. The backs of the Christmas ornaments are dated and initialed. The train pillow has a plaque on the side proclaiming that it is part of Justin's Railroad, and on the back an em-

broidered note says, *I love you. Mother, 1981.* You'll find your own ways to include your greetings and this will make each gift special.

In the Alphabet section there are several script alphabets to use if your handwriting is absolutely impossible plus several in Cross Stitch or needlepoint. There are other alphabets as part of the samplers so you should be able to compose any message you wish.

Make the most of the book. Duplicate the gifts exactly, make small color changes, or change colors completely. Some designs that are finished as crewel can just as easily be worked in needlepoint. The Locomotive Pillow Toy could be a rectangular needlepoint pillow or picture; the design for the Jacobean Needlepoint Pillow would be fine for crewel; the little counted repeats on the pincushions can be used for pillows, luggage straps, or chair seats; the Oriental Butterflies would be lovely scattered on a blouse or sweater; the contemporary Bargello could be enlarged for a stool, bench, or chair seat.

Of course this book only begins to touch on the ideas and possibilities for embroidered gifts. The graduate will appreciate the school seal worked in needlepoint or crewel and made up into a picture or pillow; every gardener will find an embroidered garden meaningful; needleworkers will use and enjoy a needle book, pincushion, or scissors case; the reader will find pleasure in a fancy book cover; sports enthusiasts cherish golf club and tennis racquet covers. The list could go on and on, and you surely have many more ideas of your own. Just remember that when you have run completely out of inspiration there is always that wonderful warm red woolen muffler!

Canvas Embroidery

A dear friend in Germany—eighty-six years old and still making beautiful needlepoint—writes fondly of boyhood memories of Tante Milly coming to visit with gifts of *broderies* which were meticulously worked and for that reason fascinating, because the designs and colors were very ugly. These were always received graciously for obviously they had been conceived with great care and represented endless time, but were always packed away the minute Tante Milly left and never reappeared until time for another visit. A "Tante Milly" became the family designation for any gift that would have a similar fate.

Most of us have had similar experiences which lead us to think carefully when planning a gift of needlework, for no matter how beautiful the present is, if it is inappropriate, it will be tucked away like a "Tante Milly." A gift of canvas embroidery is very special for it represents a great deal of time, thought and love, and those who receive such a lovely gift are truly appreciative. To facilitate choosing a suitable project for whatever occasion, the selection that follows includes basic needlepoint for pillows, pincushions, and Christmas ornaments; Bargello for eyeglass cases, pincushions, hatbands, key tags, and pillows; a textured tote on plastic canvas—all pretty, practical and too useful to hide in a drawer or closet.

Each project is shown in color as well as in a black-and-white photograph. For each there is also a chart or drawing to be traced, a list of materials needed and complete working instructions. The canvas stitches that are used for the projects are diagrammed and explained at the end of this section. Some stitches usually considered primarily for use on fabric have also been used on canvas, and these will be found with the surface stitches beginning on page 83.

MATERIALS

CANVAS

A variety of canvas weaves and mesh counts has been used in the construction of this group of articles. The list of materials with each project identifies the mesh size, weave, and color of the canvas used for that particular item. If exact duplication of the finished product is desired, the canvas should meet the specifications noted. A change to larger or smaller mesh will alter the size of the article and will invalidate the yarn requirement list.

Buy the best canvas available. It is easier to work and usually nets more attractive final results. Look at the canvas critically before buying. For plain needlepoint, the threads should be round and smooth; for Bargello it is best if the canvas is intended especially for that work and thus should have a little rougher texture which holds the upright threads in place. For any work the canvas should be without knots in the threads for these represent weak spots. Irregularities in the thickness of the threads affect the evenness of the stitches. An inferior canvas usually has a dull, flat appearance and an excess of sizing. Good quality canvas will last a long time and make more valuable the many hours' work that goes into a piece of needlepoint.

When you plan a project, allow a 2-inch border of unworked canvas on all sides of the piece. This is not a waste of canvas but an essential and functional border that helps maintain the canvas shape and makes blocking possible. It is possible to use a smaller border on some very small pieces, but it is generally a good idea to have the full 2 inches. The estimates for canvas dimensions which appear with each project in this book include these extra borders.

Tape the cut edges of the canvas with masking tape to prevent fraying and to keep the yarn from snagging on the stiff threads as the embroidery is being worked. Use only masking tape; other tapes work loose and sometimes leave a sticky deposit on the canvas.

It is important to take proper care of the canvas during the time a piece is being worked even though it looks indestructible. Keep it clean and protected by rolling it in a towel before tucking it into the work basket or bag. Avoid folding and refolding it along the same mesh as this eventually destroys the sizing in the fold and loosens the threads, making it difficult to work smooth, even stitches on that row.

Roll the canvas to fit into your hand when you are working the center—never crush and break the sizing deliberately so the canvas can be wadded into the hand. Puppies love to chew canvas and cats think it was designed for them to sleep on, so don't tempt them by leaving your work where they can find it.

FRAMES

The use of a frame in working needlepoint is optional. With a frame the work is less portable, and there may be a slight adjustment in learning to work with one hand above and the other below the frame, but the canvas maintains its shape and remains crisp and new. The stitches are usually very smooth and regular, but this is also possible without a frame. The use of the frame is therefore purely a personal decision.

A roller frame—one with or without a floor support—is best for canvas embroidery. The canvas is attached to the tapes on the rollers, and the portion not being worked on is rolled neatly out of the way. Being thus rolled is not harmful to the canvas or the finished embroidery.

Round hoops which fasten into the canvas and thus destroy the sizing are not good for this kind of work. It is best to avoid these hoops completely.

YARNS

Persian-type Yarns: The list of materials for each project contains a complete accounting of the exact yardage and colors of yarn used for the finished model. This makes duplication possible and shopping easier. Most of the yarns used are Columbia-Minerva Needlepoint and Crewel Yarn, and the color numbers that appear in the instructions are for that yarn. It is a wool yarn available in an enticing array of colors. This yarn works very well, makes lovely even stitches, does not wear thin if proper length is used, and is long wearing. The three-ply strand is convenient since the yarn can be used on large mesh canvas as it is or separated into individual strands to be used on finer work. A note at the beginning of the instructions indicates the number of strands of yarn to be used for each project.

To make the substitution of other brands of yarn possible, the yarn quantities for each project are given in yards rather than in skeins. These quantities apply to a three-ply strand regardless of the number of strands with which the stitches are to be worked. This more accurate forecasting of needs also makes it possible to use small amounts of yarn that may already be on hand. When substituting another brand of yarn, note that the replacement should be of the same weight and construction as the recommended yarn.

Yarn Requirements: The yarn requirements stated for each project are based on the amount of yarn used to complete the finished model. The quantity should be sufficient for the average careful worker to finish the piece with only a small surplus. The working methods used to determine the estimates are normal ones with no special emphasis on conservation of yarn, but no material is wasted.

There is a great variation in the ways embroiderers work and this does make yardage forecasting difficult. If you know you are extravagant with yarn or if you intend to change stitches or enlarge the piece, you will want to buy extra yarn to avoid running short before you are finished.

Whenever possible, buy all the yarn for a project at the same time. Many yarns carry a dye lot number, and there is a very slight difference in the colors from lot to lot. The frustration caused by running out of yarn of one dye lot and the hassle of trying to find more or a close-enough match are things we can all do without. Buy enough or a little extra and relax. Leftovers are always handy for spur-of-the moment projects and unopened skeins can usually be returned.

Poor Coverage of Canvas: Sometimes, even when the yarn is exactly that specified and the canvas meets the specifications too, the yarn simply does not cover the canvas properly. Try stitching with a slightly looser tension. If that does not solve the problem, separate the strands of yarn to remove the twist. If coverage is still lacking, give the yarn a steam bath by placing it in a steamer over boiling water for two or three minutes to fluff the yarn and add bulk. If all attempts fail, add an additional ply to those being used, but remember to purchase a little more as this will use up the yarn more quickly than was planned.

THIMBLE, SCISSORS, AND NEEDLES
To use a thimble or not is a purely personal decision. Its use in no way affects the quality of the embroidery. If you are accustomed to wearing one for other types of sewing, by all means use it for your canvas work; if you find it clumsy and more trouble than it is worth, forget it.

Good embroidery scissors are not a luxury. Find a pair that has tapered blades, which are sharp to the very tips, and keep them to be used for embroidery only. Protect them by keeping them in a case—an embroidered one is a good gift idea for a special person!

Keep an assortment of various sizes of tapestry needles on hand to make sure the right one is ready when you start a new project. The best size for each piece is noted in the materials list, but keep in mind that individual preferences may indicate using a size larger or a size smaller than the one recommended.

The needle for canvas embroidery should be large enough to be threaded easily with the yarn being used, and at the same time just small enough so the threaded needle passes through the mesh freely. If the needle is too large the constant abrasion will wear the yarn thin and cause it not to cover the canvas completely.

MARKING PENS
Although there is an almost bewildering assortment of marking pens, few are formulated for and suitable for use on canvas. Choose carefully. The best are labeled for use on fabric and canvas, come in several colors, are permanent and waterproof.

It is wise to test a new marker before using it. Following the instructions that come with the pen, draw on a scrap of canvas, allow it to dry, and then wet it thoroughly and dry on a white paper towel. If it is going to run or bleed, it will do so on the scrap instead of a piece of finished embroidery.

Some permanent markers are fine through the wet blocking process but react to the commonly used soil repellents for fabrics by bleeding into the yarn. If you like to use these to protect your creations, test the markers by drawing on the canvas, working a few light-colored stitches on and around the lines, then spraying with the repellent to saturate the yarn. Not all will react, but none of the pens is labeled as to safety with these sprays, and testing can save ruining a piece of finished work.

When drawing a design on canvas it is not necessary to make a heavy black line—in fact it is best to avoid just that as it will show through light-colored stitches as a dirty gray shadow! Instead of black markers, choose light blue, gray, pink, orange or light green, and look for sharp points so you can draw a fine, well-defined line. The lines need be only dark enough and heavy enough to be visible and on white canvas that is not a great deal.

If you make a mistake when drawing on the canvas, liquid typing correction fluid will cover it and dry very quickly. The fluid is also handy for making guide marks on plastic canvas.

PREPARING THE CANVAS

Always cut canvas carefully between rows of mesh and tape the raw edges to prevent fraying and to keep the yarn from snagging on the stiff threads.

TRACING THE DESIGNS

Line drawings of the exact size of the finished embroideries have been provided so there will be no enlarging problems for those who cannot draw. Large designs have been divided into sections and may be on as many as four pages. All sections have slashed dividing lines and are labeled: Upper Right Section, Lower Right Section etc., to assist in proper copying of the designs. Also, a portion of the design from the adjoining section is always shown, and these should match when the tracing is done.

It is not a good idea to lay the canvas over the page of the book and trace the design. Ink from the pen may mar the page, and it is not as easy to work on the page of the book as it is on a flat piece of paper. For this reason it is advisable to make a complete tracing of the design on paper, then lay it on a firm flat surface and trace the design onto the canvas.

To copy a design that has been divided into four quarters and is shown on four pages, fold a large piece of tracing paper into quarters. Open it flat and place it over one of the sections, matching the fold lines of the paper to the slashed lines on the drawing. Lightly trace the portion of the design shown, including the parts that overlap into the next sections. (Trace lightly so the book is not marred by impressions left by the pencil.) Move the tracing paper to the next section, match the fold lines to the slashed lines on the drawing, and the portions of this section that have already been traced will match the drawing. Trace the remainder of the section. Repeat to complete the design.

Check the full-size tracing and make certain that lines that run from one section to the next are smooth and the pattern is perfect. Go over the pencil drawing with a black felt-tipped marker so the drawing will be clear through the mesh of the canvas.

Lay the completed drawing on a flat surface. Place the taped canvas over it, centering the design so all the margins are equal. Tape or fasten the two so there is no slippage, and trace the design onto the canvas with the appropriate marker.

THE INSTRUCTIONS

With each project there is a list of materials needed, a drawing or chart, and a set of written instructions. Notes indicate the number of strands of yarn to be used, suggest working order and explain portions of the embroidery that might be more difficult than others. Following all these should produce a product not unlike the photographed model.

The suggested working order reflects my

own and indicates the best place to begin. Sometimes this is not of great importance and sometimes your own methods and tricks are of more value to you. Read the instructions through before beginning to work, look at the design carefully and decide which method is best. This way you can utilize the instructions to your own best advantage.

The freedom to change colors, stitches, and other subtleties of design is one great advantage of working from a book rather than from a purchased kit. This allows you to individualize a design and make it a personal statement. Colors can be matched exactly to existing ones, favorite stitches can be substituted, sometimes a design can be used for an entirely different purpose than the one shown.

If such changes are made, note that adjustments will have to be made in both the materials needed and the instructions. Be especially careful when changing stitches to purchase more yarn than was suggested.

THE CHARTS

Four types of needlepoint charts are included in this section on canvas embroidery. There are the freehand-style drawings which are to be traced onto the canvas; charted patterns for designs to be counted onto the canvas, charts for Bargello, and one chart for textured stitches on plastic canvas which shows stitches as they lie on the plastic.

The use of the drawings has been discussed. The Bargello charts are discussed on page 21; the instructions for the Aran Textured Tote explain the use of that chart. The designs for counted needlepoint are shown on graph paper, one square representing one stitch on the canvas. Notes on the charts make them self-explanatory and easy to follow.

OUTLINE SHADING

In several of the needlepoint pieces I have used a simple method of shading which adds a subtle dimension but does not require the artistic skill of realistic shading. The method is easy, more interesting to work than flat areas of color, and imparts a delicate blending of shades wherever it is used.

The method involves outlining a motif with one value of a color—most often it is the deepest value—then working inside that outline one row of the next lighter tone, followed by the next, etc., finally filling in the remaining space with the lightest value.

As an example, look at the oak leaf which is just above the center on the Jacobean Needlepoint Pillow. To begin the entire leaf was outlined with a single row of green 510. The vein was also worked in 510. Then a row of the next lighter green, 555, was worked inside the row of 510, following along the outline exactly. This row was followed by a row of 570; then the irregular space remaining was filled in with 575.

When an area on a needlepoint chart is marked as the oak leaf (s–510,555,570,575), this denotes that the area is to be worked in outline shading beginning with the first color listed at the outside edge, working through the colors in order, and finally filling in the remaining space with the last color.

When only two colors are listed, outline with the first and fill in the rest of the motif with the second color.

READY TO WORK

THREADING THE NEEDLE

Never wet or twist the yarn in order to thread the needle. There are three methods, one of which will work for you.

Fold method: Hold the needle between your thumb and forefinger with the eye facing you. Loop the yarn end around the needle and pull it tightly to form a fold. Holding the fold tightly, gently withdraw the needle. Still holding the fold tightly, force it through the eye of the needle.

Squeeze method: Press the end of the yarn tightly between the thumb and forefinger of one hand. With the other hand, force the eye of the needle over the tightly held yarn. With only a little practice, you will be able to fit the yarn right into the eye.

Paper method: Cut a piece of paper about an inch long and narrow enough to fit through the eye of the needle. Fold the paper in half and place the cut end of the yarn in the folded paper. Pass the folded end of the paper through the eye of the needle and the yarn will be carried through easily.

You can also buy a little wire needle threader and keep it with your work, if you prefer.

LENGTH OF YARN

The length of the strand of yarn in the needle is very important. Yarn wears thin if it is carried in and out of the canvas an excessively long time. On the other hand too many short strands are not desirable either. Generally speaking, the finer the canvas, the shorter the yarn should be. A good length to use on 10-mesh-to-the-inch canvas is 18 inches. For petit point, 8 to 10 inches is sufficient.

The needle should be in a position about 3 inches from the end of the strand of yarn. Three inches is enough to anchor the needle so it will not slip off the yarn, but makes carrying a double strand of yarn through the canvas necessary for a short time. This saves wear on the yarn.

WORKING WITH THE TWIST OF THE YARN

If you pull a strand of Persian-type yarn through your fingers in one direction, you will feel a slight roughness, while the yarn feels smooth if you pull in the opposite direction. Smoother stitches will be the result if the yarn is always threaded into the needle so that the smooth side follows the needle into the canvas.

YARN TWISTING AND WEARING THIN

If the yarn becomes twisted as you work—a natural occurrence—hold the canvas up, drop the needle, and let the yarn unwind itself. Do not continue to work with the twisted yarn; it will not cover the canvas well and the stitches will have a slightly different shape as a result of the twist.

It is possible to prevent the yarn from twisting while working. As the needle is drawn out of the canvas at the completion of a stitch, roll it about a quarter-turn in the direction of the canvas. A little pressure from the thumb is all it takes to do this and it quickly becomes an automatic gesture. It may seem too simple to work, but it does!

If the yarn wears thin before you reach the end of a strand even when the proper short length is being used, change needles. Try a size smaller or change to another brand.

Though all the eyes look alike, some are shaped in a manner that causes them to cut the yarn.

WASTE KNOT

A permanent knot of any type left in canvas embroidery will make a raised spot on the surface, making it impossible to achieve the smooth, even surface needed for good appearance.

The Waste Knot, however, which is temporary and removed after it has served its purpose, can often solve the problem of anchoring a strand of yarn when there is nothing in which to fasten it. This is sometimes the case in a completely blank new canvas or with Bargello since the stitches are so long.

In these cases, make a knot in the end of the strand of yarn. Take the needle down into the canvas from the right side about 3 inches from the place the first stitch will be. Place the knot also in a position relative to the first stitch so that subsequent stitches will go through the strand on the back and eventually fasten it. Usually five or six stitches are sufficient. When the strand holding the knot is sufficiently anchored, cut the knot off the top of the canvas and trim the remaining thread on the back. There will be no trace of the knot and the first stitch will be firmly fastened.

BEGINNING AND ENDING A STRAND OF YARN

Attach the yarn for the first few stitches on a canvas either with a Waste Knot or simply by holding the end of the yarn on the back and working through it until it is fastened. Begin subsequent strands by pulling them through the back of the last four or five stitches worked.

End a strand of yarn by pulling it through the back of four or five stitches in the row above. Never begin and end in the same group of stitches as this pulls the stitches tightly on the right side and causes a ridge that will not block out.

Clip all ends short to avoid tangling and to keep them from being pulled to the right side when new stitches are worked around them. This is particularly important when a number of different colors is being used.

MISTAKES

A good needleworker is a good ripper. It is a mistake to leave a flaw in your work. It will always be obvious to you even if no one else seems to notice. Ripping may be tedious and dull work, but it is always worthwhile and results in an improvement. Don't let anyone convince you that a few mistakes add charm to your work. Try from the beginning to make every stitch perfect, and when you find one that is not right, pick it out and replace it with a good stitch. You will be much happier in the end.

BARGELLO

Bargello is a counted canvas embroidery worked primarily in the Upright Gobelin or Bargello Stitch and the basic rules for good needlepoint apply to it. These further hints should be added specifically for Bargello.

Count the Bargello stitches carefully, following the given chart until the pattern is established. Accuracy is essential, for very often a line or lines delineate a pattern and all other rows merely follow. If a mistake is made in the first row, it will carry into all subsequent rows. Do not waste time trying to work around an error. The more effort you put into trying to work around a mistake, the worse it will become.

Since Bargello stitches are long, they use up yarn quickly, and so it is possible to work with a longer strand of yarn than is generally used for other needlepoint stitches. A length of 15 to 18 inches is usually comfortable. Greater lengths are hard to handle and will wear thin before they are stitched in.

Learn to work the Bargello stitches with a light, even tension. The stitches lie upright on the canvas and must be loose enough to allow the yarn to "fluff" up and cover the canvas. If the canvas threads are visible between the stitches, either the stitches are too tight or the yarn is not heavy enough to cover the canvas being used. Try stitching with a lighter tension. If that does not solve the problem, try one of the methods of increasing the bulk described on page 16.

Bargello stitches should lie flat on the canvas with no twisting of the yarn on the right side of the embroidery. Take time to guide the yarn into a perfect stitch every time. The smooth, even surface that results enhances the beauty of Bargello designs.

There are several very good canvases made especially for Bargello. Most are either ecru or pale cream in color and are a mono weave with threads that are slightly fuzzy. This makes a good surface for the embroidery as the roughness of the threads seems to hold the yarn in place, and there is usually little problem with canvas specks showing between stitches. Mono canvas is generally acceptable for Bargello and some of the interlocking mono weaves can be used successfully, but this depends completely on the weave of the particular canvas. Some are fine while others hold the stitches apart and just can't be used.

THE BARGELLO CHARTS

Although rendered in black and white, the Bargello charts are very clear and look very much like the finished embroidery. They are drawn on graph paper, the stitches shown outlined in black with a color symbol within the outline. A color key relates the symbols to the yarn colors.

When a stitch is drawn to enclose four squares, this indicates the stitch is to be worked over four canvas threads—count threads, not holes. Stitches drawn to enclose two squares are two threads long, etc.

Generally a discussion in the instructions will point out the best place to begin work and establish the pattern. Notes on the charts themselves point out the center rows and give other clues to make following the design easy.

THE CANVAS STITCHES

Canvas stitches that are worked over the threads of the canvas in a regular, exacting, and repetitive manner are, as a result, very soothing and relaxing once they have been mastered. There is nothing quite as soothing as the quiet rhythm of the Basket Weave Stitch; nothing else takes one's mind away from problems as completely as an intricate counted pattern—the hours fly by with either the complicated or the plain.

There are hundreds of stitches and variations of stitches—all interesting to work and some more useful than others. There is a story behind most stitches, a little bit of history or legend that lends a touch of romance and adds to the pleasures of embroidery. Some needleworkers become greatly involved in this aspect of the stitches; others are intrigued purely by the stitches themselves and the beauty and interest they add to the embroidery. Either way, we all come to enjoy these fascinating and varied stitches and eventually we all experiment with them.

The stitches that follow are just a sampling of the many canvas stitches—the basic and versatile Tent Stitch and a few fancy ones that have been used to make the designs in the book. You may wish to add others—and, indeed, that is one advantage you gain from using the designs in a book—in order to personalize the designs by changing either stitches or colors or both. You may prefer to work the green border of the Peking Butterfly Pillow entirely in a textured stitch instead of the Basket Weave shown; or you may want to add dimension to the Jacobean Needlepoint Pillow by adding crewel stitches on top of the needlepoint to turn it into crewelpoint. The options are yours.

The stitch charts that follow are simple and easy to use. The grid background represents the canvas and the stitches are shown as they will be on the canvas. The only way to learn a stitch is to actually work it. Thread a needle, examine the chart, read the written instructions, and then follow the instructions step-by-step to the completion of the stitch. Always bring the needle to the surface from the back of the canvas in the space with the number 1, go to the back at 2 and come back to the surface at 3. Place the needle as shown and the stitch should work out correctly every time.

TENT STITCH

This is *the* needlepoint stitch, the basic and versatile stitch that is the backbone of most canvas embroidery. It is an oval stitch that always slants upward from lower left to upper right and fits so closely to its neighbors that it completely covers the canvas and creates that prized fabric which is needlepoint.

The two best methods for making the Tent Stitch—the Basket Weave and the Continental—are probably familiar to all readers but are diagrammed here for reference. Although it is best to work as much as possible in the Basket Weave, the two stitches require similar amounts of yarn and may be interchanged freely. The Basket Weave causes less distortion of canvas, and therefore is less of a problem to block and much favored by most needleworkers.

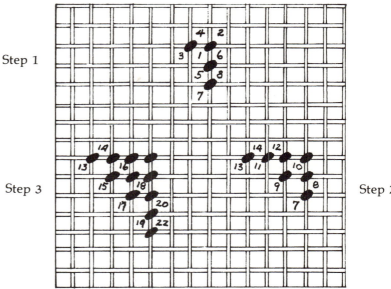

Step 1

Step 3

Step 2

BASKET WEAVE STITCH

Try the Basket Weave Stitch first within the confines of a square shape until you understand the stitching routine; then try working an irregular shape. Often it is helpful to outline an irregular shape with a row of Continental and then work the Basket Weave within the outline.

The Basket Weave is worked in diagonal rows beginning at the top right corner of the canvas. The rows alternate, one row worked in an upward direction and the next worked downward.

Practice on a small piece of canvas beginning at the upper right corner with the first stitch and follow the numbered sequence in Step 1 to place the first four stitches. Note that when the needle goes down at *8* in the last stitch of Step 1 it passes under two vertical threads to come up at *9* in Step 2. This is always true on the upward row as you will notice in the next two stitches. On this row the needle is in a horizontal position. The last stitch of Step 2 is actually the first stitch of the next row. Note its position on the same horizontal thread as the previous stitch.

Step 3 is a downward diagonal row and these stitches are made with the needle in a vertical position. Note again that the needle always passes under two threads but this time it is two horizontal threads. The last stitch on the Step 3 chart is the first stitch in the next row, and it lies directly under the previous stitch. The next row is worked upward as in Step 2, and these two rows alternate throughout the work. After several rows the distinctive woven pattern appears on the back.

Step 1

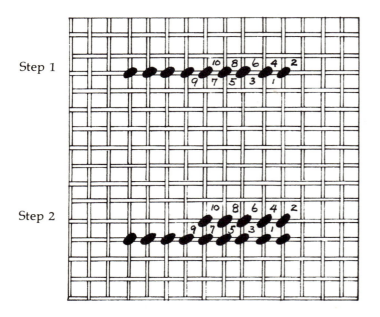

Step 2

CONTINENTAL STITCH
The Continental Stitch is worked in rows across the canvas beginning at the top right corner. Work the first row in the numbered sequence shown by Step 1. When the end of the row is reached turn the canvas completely around, so the top is now the bottom, and work the next row as in Step 2.

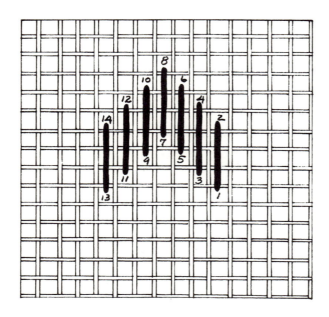

BARGELLO STITCH
The Bargello Stitch is really the Upright Gobelin Stitch worked in steps up and down across the row to create the familiar flame pattern. The simple stitch can be placed on the canvas to form many beautiful patterns. Work the stitches with a light, even tension so the yarn covers the canvas completely. See page 20 for tips on Bargello.

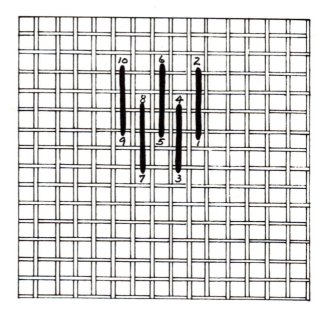

BRICK STITCH

The Brick Stitch is the Upright Gobelin again, this time arranged so that the stitches are alternately two threads up and two down, creating the "brick" pattern. This stitch works very quickly, and the stitches should be made loosely so the yarn will cover the canvas. The length of the stitches can be varied according to the effect needed. Shown on the chart they are worked over four threads, but they can easily be six or two threads in length and still be very attractive.

DOUBLE STRAIGHT CROSS STITCH

The development of a stitch is always interesting. This one is made up of an upright cross held in place by a smaller traditional Cross Stitch. The effect is a neat, slightly raised stitch.

To fill a slightly larger space, the variation that begins with an upright cross worked over six threads rather than two is a good substitution. Note also that the variation has two smaller crosses with longer arms to completely cover its diamond space. This is a wonderful texture to add to projects like the Aran Textured Tote on page 53.

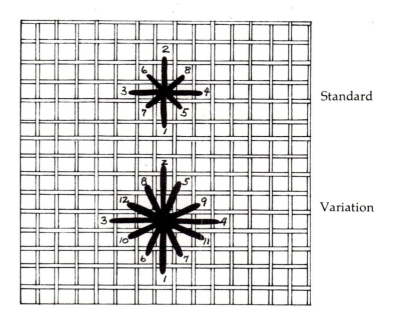

Standard

Variation

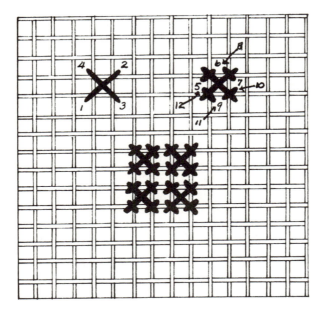

RICE STITCH

Although a bit tedious to work, the Rice Stitch has a good, smooth surface and a most attractive texture and pattern. It is basically a Cross Stitch with a small diagonal stitch tying down each of the corners. It is interesting to make the crosses of one color and to use a contrasting color to tie down the arms. The diagram shows first the sequence of stitches to form the basic cross, then the tie-down stitches, and finally a group of four finished stitches shows the way the stitches fit together.

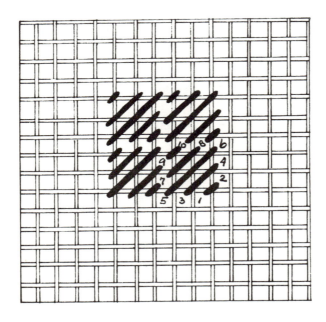

SCOTCH STITCH

This is one of the best known and widely used of the decorative stitches. As shown in the diagram the stitch has been worked over a square of three threads of canvas. A larger square of pattern can be made by making one more stitch—one thread longer—in the center before decreasing to the smaller stitches in the sequence. A big area worked in this stitch will distort the canvas badly, but it can generally be blocked out without much problem.

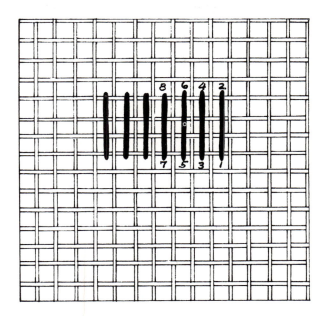

UPRIGHT GOBELIN STITCH

The Upright Gobelin Stitch produces very pronounced horizontal rows of pattern, covers ground very quickly and makes the kind of background that adds texture but does not overpower the design itself. The stitch can be worked over a varying number of threads depending on how wide a stripe of stitches is needed.

28

JACOBEAN NEEDLEPOINT PILLOW

Jacobean designs like this one are most often found in crewel embroidery, but with its traditional fanciful bird and flowers this one adapts beautifully to 14-mesh canvas embroidery. An easy method of outline shading adds a delicate dimension, and the range of colors adapts to almost any color scheme.

A piece of fine needlepoint is a truly exceptional gift for one who will appreciate the careful craftsmanship and many hours that went into its making. Personalize the piece by adding your initials and the date in the

lower corner. If the pillow marks a landmark date—Golden Anniversary, Wedding, New House, etc.—you can embroider the occasion, the celebrants' names and the date on the pillow back as a permanent remembrance.

If you prefer crewel to needlepoint, use the design for an embroidery pattern. Use the colors suggested on a natural linen background and choose your own stitches. It will be an interesting project.

JACOBEAN NEEDLEPOINT PILLOW

Upper Left Section

Upper Right Section

Lower Left Section

JACOBEAN NEEDLEPOINT PILLOW

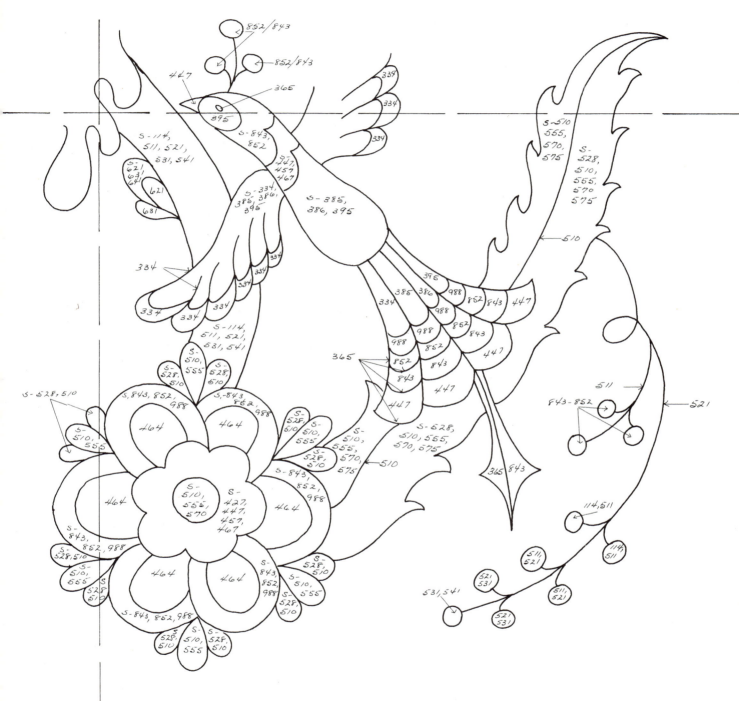

Lower Right Section

FINISHED SIZE
14 × 14 inches

MATERIALS
  #14 white mono canvas, 18 × 18 inches
  #20 tapestry needle
  Persian yarn as follows: 015, Antique White, 125 yards; 395, Light Blue, 3 yards; 386, Blue Balloon, 3 yards; 385, French Blue, 3 yards; 334, Dark French Blue, 4 yards; 365, French Navy, 3 yards; 575, Spring Pea Green, 8 yards; 570, Celery Leaf, 5 yards; 555, Green Giant, 7 yards; 510, Medium Green, 10 yards; 528, Forest Green, 4 yards; 438, Buttercup, 4 yards; 467, Light Medium Yellow, 4 yards; 457, Canary Yellow, 3 yards; 447, Mustard, 4 yards; 427, Medium Gold, 4 yards; 464, Orange Ice, 5 yards; 988, Peach, 5 yards; 852, Coral, 7 yards; 843, Fire Ball, 9 yards; 541, Golden Sands, 4 yards; 531, Empire Gold, 6 yards; 521, Earth, 7 yards; 511, Pecan, 8 yards; 114, Deep Brown, 3 yards; 641, Light Mauve, 2 yards; 631, Light Iris, 3 yards; 621, Aster, 2 yards
  Appropriate fabric for pillow back, ½ yard

NOTE
Separate the yarn and work all needlepoint with two ply.

INSTRUCTIONS
When I am working an entire piece in Tent Stitch I use the Basket Weave whenever possible. There is less distortion of the canvas and the result is usually a prettier piece of work. The yarn quantities have been computed on the basis of Basket Weave, but you can safely switch to the Continental if you prefer it as they require the same amounts of yarn.

Following the instructions on page 17, trace the four sections of the design and join them to form a 14-inch square. Using the guidelines on one of the sections, mark the center of the design. Also mark the center of the canvas piece. Measuring out from the center of the canvas, outline a 14-inch square. Center the design on the square, and with a waterproof pen trace the design onto the canvas. Tape the edges.

Outline shading is indicated when the letter s and several numbers appear on a motif on the chart. Use the first color noted to outline the motif; then work one row just inside the first with the next color listed, continuing to use the colors in order, filling in all remaining space with the last color.

When only one color number appears in a motif, work that entire area in just that color. Work all background in 015, Antique White.

Begin working on the oak leaf just above the center of the design. Outline the entire leaf and work the vein in color 510. Next work a row of 555 inside the outline. Follow with a row of 570. Finally fill in all the remaining space with 575.

Next work the wide gold stem sections above and below the oak leaf, beginning with a row of 511 on both right and left sides. Follow with rows of 521 and 531. Fill in the center with 541.

At this point, some comments about working order are probably useful. Most of you already have established patterns by which you work and complete pieces like this. It is usually my preference to begin working the design at or near the center and to work out toward the sides. At the same time I like to start the background at the upper right corner and work small amounts of it at a time so I am not left with all of it at the end. On this piece, after the oak leaf and stem have been worked, I would progress upward to the center flower, to the butterfly, and then to the carnation directly below it. This would allow me to keep the background going and keep the canvas in better shape. If you work in this manner, you will be able to keep the pattern of the Basket Weave background and never have to join two rows in the same direction and accept the resulting misweave.

Working in this direction would lead me next to the bird. Work the pale blue face, gold bill and eye. Outline the hood with a row of 843 and proceed to finish shading as indicated. Work the plumes of the crest and a few of the stitches at the base of each circular feather with 842. Round out the feathers with 852. Work gold neck section. Outline the wings including the feather lines and solid scalloped tips with 334. Shade only along the curved top edges with rows of 385 and 386; then fill in the remaining space with 395. Work the body section shading with the blues noted. The top narrow portion of the tail is divided into four solid areas as indicated. Outline the flaring tail feathers and all the little curved sections with 365. Then fill in the areas with the colors noted. The single pointed tail feather is solid 365 and 843.

When two numbers appear on a berry, work three or four stitches with the darker color at the base near the stem, then round out the berry with the lighter color. Don't try to make all berries exactly alike—the variations make them prettier.

Leave the butterfly's antennae until after the background has been worked. Then, using a single strand of 114, just make two straight stitches on top of the background to indicate antennae.

The balance of the piece is worked in the same manner as that which has been outlined. When the needlepoint is complete, block and finish it as a pillow.

GEOMETRIC NEEDLEPOINT PINCUSHIONS

Just for fun—little remembrances, thank you's, hostess gifts, stocking stuffers—whenever a tiny but special offering is needed, here are two little pincushions in geometric needlepoint designs.

The designs are also a handy reference for patterns for pillows, luggage straps, book covers, chair seats, eyeglass cases—anywhere a repeat design can be used. Each will also adapt neatly for a border to finish off or enlarge a small piece. Large mesh canvas will enlarge the size of the repeat without destroying the classic feeling.

Pastel Pincushion

FINISHED SIZE
4¼ × 4¼ inches

MATERIALS
#14 white mono canvas, 8 × 8 inches
#20 tapestry needle
Persian yarn as follows: 005, White, 7 yards; 532, Lettuce, 6 yards; 281, Antique Pink, 4 yards (additional 281 for twisted cord and tassels, 3 yards)
Fabric for backing, approximately 6 × 6 inches
Small amount of fiberfilling

NOTE
Use two ply of the yarn and Tent Stitch throughout.

INSTRUCTIONS
Tape the canvas and mark the center. Begin working at the center, placing the center square noted on the chart in the center of the canvas. Work out from the center in any order that's easy for you and work four complete squares. Work three rows of white at the outside edges to finish.

Block and finish as shown with a twisted cord and tassels, or edge with lace or self-piping.

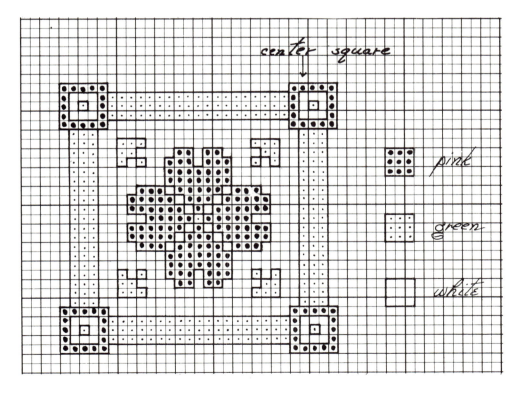

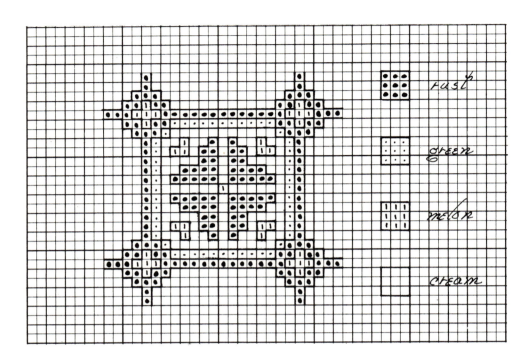

Classic Pincushion

FINISHED SIZE
4 × 4 inches

MATERIALS
  #14 white mono canvas, 7 × 7 inches
  #20 tapestry needle
  Persian yarn as follows: 464, Orange Ice, 5
    yards; 273, Light Terra Cotta, 2 yards;
    555, Green Giant, 5 yards; 414, Rust, 6
    yards (additional 414 for twisted cord
    and tassel, 4 yards)
  Fabric for backing, approximately 5 × 5
    inches
  Small amount of fiberfilling

NOTE
Use two ply of the yarn and Tent Stitch
throughout.

INSTRUCTIONS
Tape the canvas and mark the center. The
chart shows one motif and the beginnings of
the connecting outlines for its neighbors.
Since the pincushion is made of three rows
of three motifs each, the center of the motif
graphed should be placed in the center of the
canvas. Begin working at the center and
work outward in an order that's convenient
for you.

  Work nine motifs to form a square. Add
three rows of 464 at the outside edge to form
a border. Block and finish as shown with a
twisted cord of rust and one fat tassel at one
corner.

BUTTERFLY GRAPHIC

Always a favorite, the butterfly in a big bold design and bright colors on large mesh canvas creates a memorable needlepoint pillow or picture. The cheerful combination of colors will fit into most decorating schemes and makes this a most welcome gift.

The graphic design can also be worked entirely in black and white as shown in the small picture. This is a very striking effect and an answer to many contemporary needs.

40

FINISHED SIZE
14 × 14 inches

MATERIALS

#12 white mono canvas, 18 × 18 inches
#18 or #19 tapestry needle
Persian Yarn as follows: 405, Copper, 55 yards; 456, Baby Yellow, 25 yards; 970, Light Orange, 4 yards; 570, Celery Leaf, 12 yards; 555, Green Giant, 14 yards; 510, Medium Green, 8 yards; 520, Hunter Green, 8 yards; 528, Forest Green, 6 yards; 765, Light Teal, 5 yards; 760, Aquamarine, 5 yards; 783, Medium Teal, 6 yards; 755, Caribbean Blue, 10 yards; 464, Orange Ice, 4 yards; 988, Peach, 5 yards; 852, Coral, 11 yards; 843, Fire Ball, 5 yards; 012, Ivory, 55 yards
Appropriate fabric for pillow back, ½ yard

NOTE
Separate the yarn and work all stitches with two strands.

INSTRUCTIONS
Fold a piece of tracing paper into quarters. Open it flat and place it over the drawing, matching fold lines to the dashed lines on the drawing. Trace both sections of the butterfly. Fold the paper in half and trace the outlines to complete the design.

Tape the canvas edges. Find the center of the canvas and draw a horizontal and a vertical line through the center mark to divide the canvas into quarters. Lay the canvas over the drawing, matching the lines on the canvas to the fold lines on the drawing. With a waterproof marker trace the butterfly onto the canvas.

Measure out 6 inches from the center at the top, bottom, and sides, and draw a line to indicate the beginning of the border stitching.

Note that the model photographed was worked with two strands of Persian yarn, and the yarn quantities were based on the use of only two strands. Coverage is adequate with this yarn, but brands differ slightly and if yours does not cover the canvas well, try steaming the yarn as explained on page 16. If that does not solve the problem, switch to the full three ply, but be sure to buy at least one third more to be certain you will have enough to finish.

Work completely in Tent Stitch except for the row of Scotch Stitch in the border. Use Basket Weave as much as possible to keep the canvas straight. When an area is marked to indicate that two yarn colors were used (783/760), outline the motif with a single line of the first color, then fill it in completely with the second color.

Complete the butterfly. Outline the marked square with a single row of 510, Medium Green. Count the stitches of this row and make the square 161 × 161. If your outlined square does not count this number of stitches exactly, adjust it so the row of Scotch Stitch squares that follows later will fit.

Next, work two rows of Tent Stitch outside the green row, using 852, Coral. Follow with one row of Scotch Stitch squares in 405, Copper, working each square over five mesh and alternating the slant of the stitches from square to square. Finish with two rows of 405, Copper, Tent Stitch.

Fill in the background with 012, Ivory and plain Basket Weave. Block and complete as a pillow or picture.

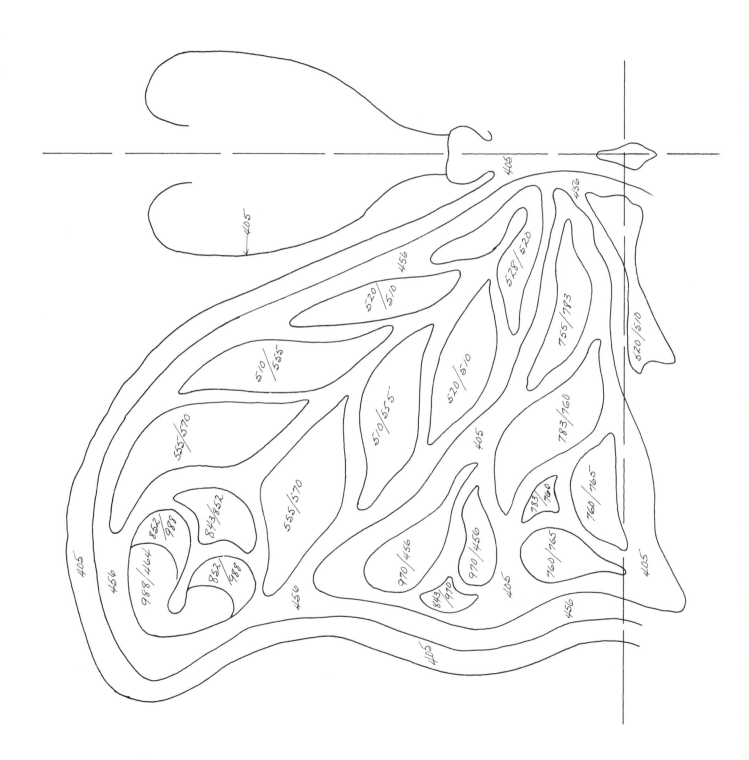

BUTTERFLY GRAPHIC

Top Section

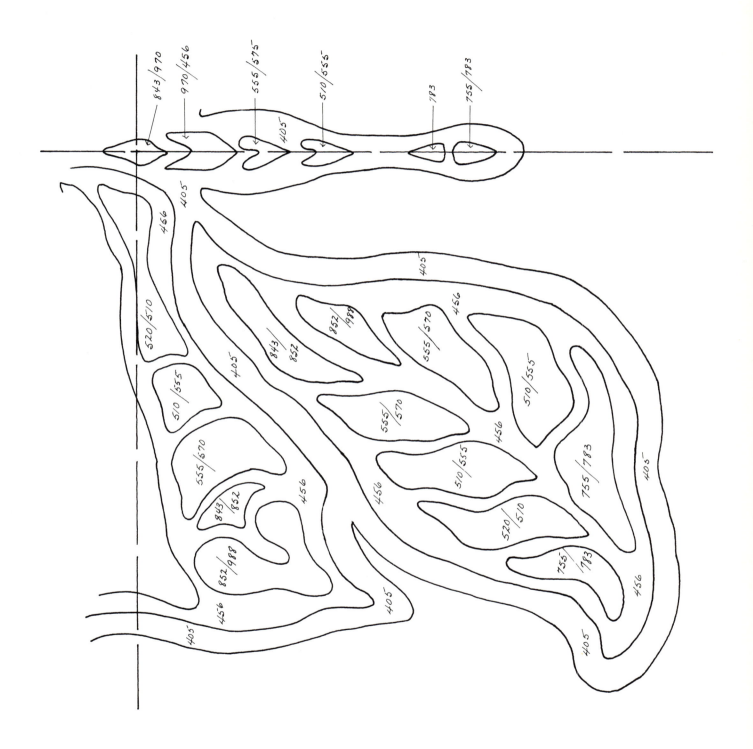

Bottom Section

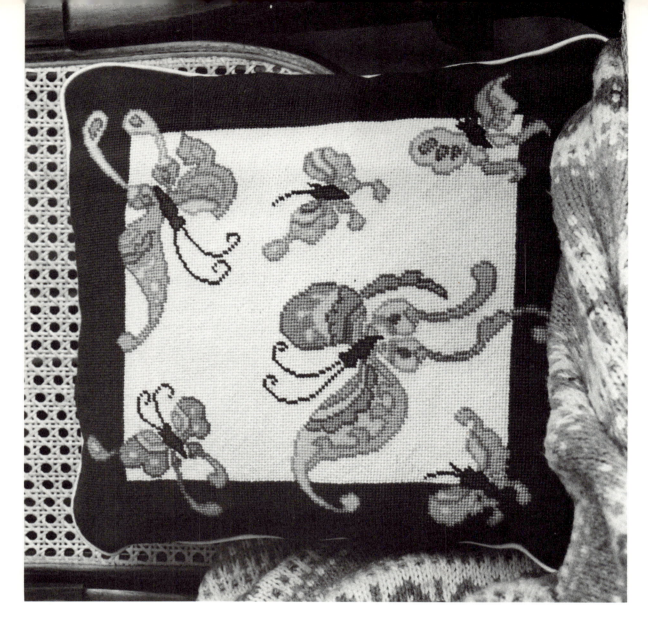

PEKING BUTTERFLIES

For those who prefer needlepoint to crewel embroidery, here are the Chinese butterflies translated for canvas work. The butterflies are slightly enlarged, and this colorful rendition uses bright pastels on a snowy white background and Shamrock Green border. Tent Stitch has been used throughout on the finished model and the yarn quantities are for that stitch, but it would be interesting to use a textured stitch—my choice would be Rice Stitch—for the green border.

Flat areas of color are enlivened by an outline of a darker shade of each color— pink is edged with deeper pink, blue by darker blue, yellow with orange. This is a pretty pillow that will make a most welcome gift. Put your initials and the date in light green in the lower right corner of the border. You can, if you wish, use one of the alphabets on pages 150, 152 to add the recipient's name across the top border.

44

FINISHED SIZE
13½ × 13½ inches

MATERIALS
#14 white mono canvas, 18 × 18 inches
#20 tapestry needle
Persian yarn as follows: 005, White, 60 yards; G-54, Shamrock Green, 70 yards; R-70 Frosted Cherry, 5 yards; 860, Magnolia, 7 yards; 975, Pumpkin, 7 yards; 456, Baby Yellow, 9 yards; 752, Medium Blue, 7 yards; 756, Summer Blue, 7 yards; 217, Wood Brown, 3 yards; 247, Clove Brown, 4 yards; G-64, Spring Apple Green, 4 yards; G-74, Light Apple Green, 6 yards

Appropriate fabric for the pillow back, ½ yard

NOTE
The pillow is worked entirely in Basket Weave Stitch, and yarn quantities are computed on the basis of that stitch. Separate the yarn and work Basket Weave Stitch with two strands throughout.

INSTRUCTIONS
Fold a piece of tracing paper in half vertically. Open the paper flat and match the fold line to the slashed lines on the charts. Trace both sides of the design, using partial butterflies and border lines as guides in lining up the two halves. Cut the canvas to size and bind the edges to prevent fraying. Lay the canvas over the tracing and with a permanent ink marker, trace the design and border line onto the canvas. Measure out 2 inches on all sides from the traced border lines and draw another line to mark the outside edge of the border. The piece should measure 13½ × 13½ inches.

Wherever possible work in the Basket Weave Stitch. You will have to work the outlines around motifs mostly in Continental, but all areas can be filled in with Basket Weave.

All parts of the butterflies are outlined with a darker shade of one color and filled in with another. When the chart shows the two numbers with a slash (/) between them, outline with the first and fill in with the second.

My working order for this piece is to start in the upper right corner with the green border and work down to the butterfly in that corner. Then I work the butterfly, and at the same time I keep working the background around it. I work a little background at a time to keep the canvas in shape and avoid having to work all the dull part at one time. Be careful to keep the sequence of the Basket Weave rows intact so you do not have ugly diagonal lines running across the finished canvas.

Block the completed needlepoint and make it up into a pillow following the instructions on page 155.

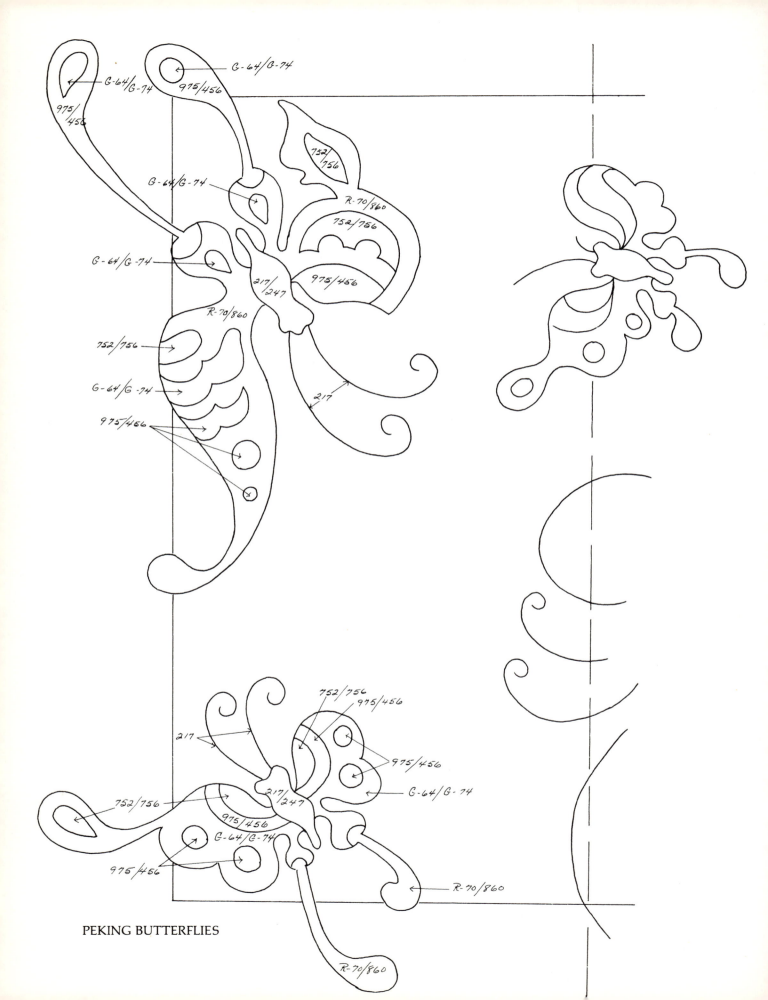

PEKING BUTTERFLIES

CHRISTMAS SNOWFLAKES

Handmade ornaments on the tree have a nostalgic charm that is hard to duplicate. It will take quite a number to decorate the entire tree, but a collection can begin with just a few the first year and an annual addition until the tree is filled with treasures.

Begin with these little squares decorated with snowflakes and worked on easy-to-handle #12 canvas. Each of the four designs can be worked in a number of colors so you

really have ideas for a variety of ornaments on this page.

Give the newlyweds four ornaments as the nucleus of their Christmas collection. If the bride is not a needleworker, you may inspire her to learn needlepoint to continue to build their collection. If not, you can add a few every year as an early Christmas present and the beginning of a happy tradition.

48

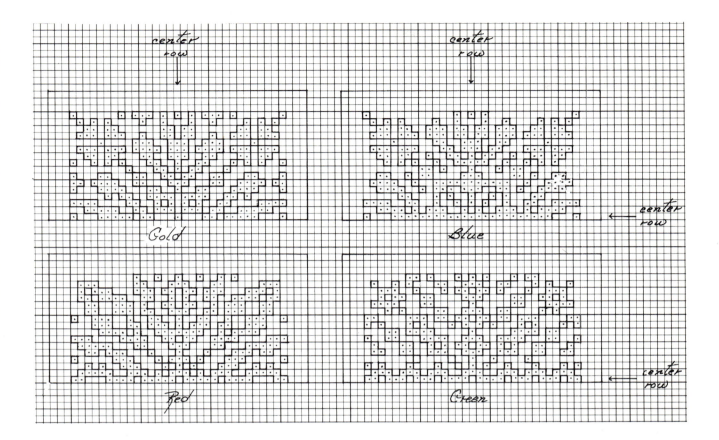

FINISHED SIZE
3 × 3 inches

MATERIALS
 #12 white mono canvas, 7 × 7 inches for
 each ornament
 #18 or #19 tapestry needle
 Persian yarn as follows: Christmas red,
 blue, gold or green, 10 yards per ornament; white, 8 yards per ornament
 Metallic gold yarn, approximately 2 yards
 per ornament
 Felt in colors to match yarns, a 4-inch
 square for each ornament
 Fiber filling, a generous handful

NOTE
Work the needlepoint with the three-ply
strand of yarn.
 Ornaments as shown have only one side
worked in needlepoint and are backed with
felt in a matching color. They would be extra
attractive if both sides were needlepoint.
Add more to yarn quantities if you opt for
this construction.

INSTRUCTIONS

Cut the canvas to size and tape the edges. Work the entire white snowflake design— shown by the dotted pattern on the graph— beginning at any point in the design that is convenient for you. Fill in the background and block it.

Trim the unworked canvas borders to ½ inch. Cut the felt to the same size as the trimmed canvas. With a steam iron, turn back the unworked borders and press in place. Turn back part of the last row of stitches so no unworked canvas will show in the finished ornament.

Cut a piece of cardboard 1½ inches wide. Make a small tassel from the metallic yarn by winding it around the cardboard six times and tying it at the top, again at a point just below the top, and trimming the bottom to a straight edge. Leave the tie ends at the top long enough to use them to attach the tassel to the canvas.

Make a twisted cord to trim the side edges by cutting a 48-inch length of the metallic yarn. Double the yarn in half, hold both ends and twist it tightly. Holding the two ends firmly, double the twisted yarn and let

go of the end. The yarn will twist back against itself to form a twisted cord. Tie the cut ends tightly and the cord will stay twisted.

Cut a 3-inch strand of the metallic yarn and attach it to the top of the worked ornament to form a hanger loop. I just thread it into a needle, run it into the corner, and then tie the ends together. Attach the tassel to the opposite corner in the same manner.

Turn back ½ inch on all sides of the felt, and with right sides together and beginning at the top corner of the ornament, using matching sewing thread, whip the two together leaving about 1 inch open at the end. Stuff with a small amount of fiber filling and close the opening except for a tiny space at the very end, just large enough to tuck the ends of the twisted cord into in the next step.

Tuck one end of the metallic cord into the opening at the top of the ornament, and whip the cord to the side of the ornament with long stitches, using the sewing thread. If the stitches slant they will fall into the twist of the cord and be almost invisible. Tuck the end into the top and fasten off the thread.

CHRISTMAS CRYSTALS

The elongated diamond shape of these ornaments mixes well with the square Christmas Snowflakes to make a pretty tree. The ornaments are so small you can use up odds and ends of yarn and make them up in an excit-ing array of colors. To personalize, use a piece of graph paper and one of the charted alphabets to plan the recipient's initials or the date, and work it in needlepoint for the back of one of the ornaments.

FINISHED SIZE
2¼ × 3½ inches

MATERIALS
   #12 white mono canvas, 6 × 7 inches for
      each ornament
   #18 or #19 tapestry needle
   Persian yarn as follows: Christmas red,
      blue, gold or green, 8 yards per orna-
      ment; .white, 7 yards per ornament
   Metallic gold yarn, approximately 2 yards
      per ornament
   Felt in colors to match yarns, a piece about
      3 × 4½ inches for each ornament
   Fiberfilling, a generous handful

NOTE
Work the needlepoint with the three-ply
strand of yarn.

   Ornaments shown have only one side
worked in needlepoint and are backed in felt
in a matching color. They would be extra attractive if both sides were needlepoint, either
in the same design or personalized as suggested above. Add more to the yarn quantities if you opt for this construction.

INSTRUCTIONS
Work the needlepoint and construct as in
the directions for Christmas Snowflakes on
page 50.

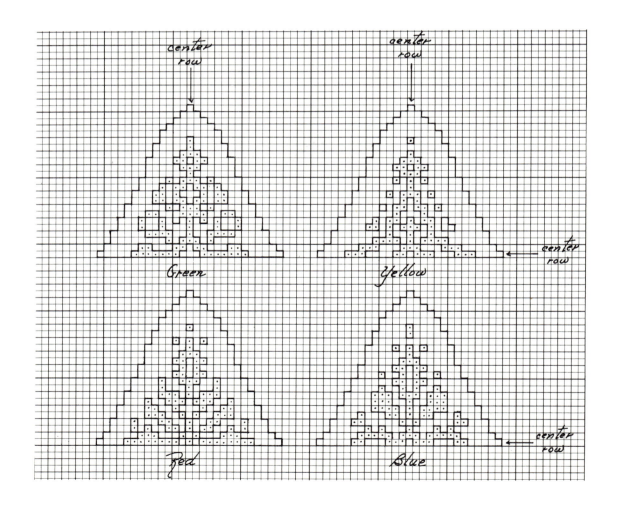

ARAN TEXTURED TOTE

The creamy color and the interplay of stitches and textures on this bag recall that of the distinctive fisherman knits from the tiny island of Aran. A double strand of knitting worsted on 7-mesh-to-the-inch canvas creates the handsome mixture of patterns while the plastic "canvas" provides a firm but flexible foundation for a practical and individual gift.

FINISHED SIZE
10½ × 13 × 3 inches

MATERIALS
  Three sheets of plastic canvas, 10½ × 13½ inches
  Knitting worsted weight yarn, two 4-ounce skeins (containing 280 yards each) in winter white or a pale cream color
  Tapestry needle
  Fabric for lining, ½ yard

NOTE
Work throughout with a double strand of yarn.

INSTRUCTIONS

The plastic sheets are 70 holes by 90 holes. Use one full sheet each for the front and back pieces. The pattern requires that these two pieces be 70 holes by 87 holes. The extra plastic can be cut off after the pieces are worked.

Cut the third piece of plastic to make the side panels, bottom and handles. Cutting across the width of the piece, cut three pieces the full 90-mesh width and 19 holes wide. Trim one to 87 holes for the bottom. Trim the other two to measure 70 holes by 19 holes for the side panels. From the remaining strip cut two handles 90 × 4. Always count holes when cutting sections.

The diagram shows the stitches exactly as they lie on the canvas, the lines on the chart representing the plastic mesh. To simplify the chart somewhat, I've shown only the foundation spokes of the Spider Webs, and only one of each of the other raised stitches is drawn. These stitches are then indicated in the open spaces by letters and are further diagrammed at the side. Rice, Continental and Scotch Stitches lie on the canvas as shown.

To aid in working, the Double Straight Cross variation and the Bump Stitch (this one used in two sizes and indicated by *D* and *E* on the chart) are diagrammed and numbered on the side of the chart. Work them as for the other diagrammed canvas stitches, following the numbers in the order shown. Note that the Double Straight Cross Stitch charted on page 25 is shown as traditionally worked over four threads with four stitches making the pattern while the variation used on the tote is worked over six threads with six stitches forming the diamond.

As far as I know the Bump Stitch is really not a stitch at all and thus has no name, but I needed something to call this collection of stitches which forms a nice raised square. Work the diagonal stitches as shown across six mesh and follow the numbers in rhythmic order to form the square. Always work the stitches in the same sequence so the top ones all slant in the same direction.

The small version of the Bump (*E*) is outlined with a row of Continental and then the Bump is worked over four mesh. Reverse the stitching order so the top stitches slant in the opposite direction from those on the larger Bumps.

Sometimes the Spider Webs do not cover the canvas completely at the outside edges of the stitch. You can remedy this by working a row of Continental Stitch around the square and then placing the foundation stitches for the spokes over the Continental.

I'd begin to work at the top right corner, working the Upright Gobelin row, then laying the foundation of star shapes. Another order may appeal to you more. When working with the double strand of yarn, keep the strands flat so the stitches are smooth.

Work the front, back, and side panels as charted. Work the bottom in Brick Stitch. For the handles, use the slanted stitches as shown; then with the double strand work an overcasting stitch on the edges to cover the exposed bar.

Using the plastic pieces as patterns, cut the lining, adding a 5/8-inch seam allowance on all sides. Sew the seams. Press. Turn the seam allowance at the top edge of the lining to the wrong side and press it in place.

Matching the holes of the adjoining pieces, join the bag sections with an overcasting stitch. Finish the top edge of the bag with the same overcasting stitch. Attach the bag handles, placing the ends about 3 inches from the outside corners. Sew a narrow strip of lining material to the wrong side of the handles to finish them.

Insert the lining into the bag and fasten it along the top with invisible stitches.

Stitches

A   Spider Web, Whipped
B   Spider Web, Woven
C   Double Straight Cross Stitch
D   Bump Stitch
E   Bump Stitch Outlined by Continental
F   Rice
G   Scotch
H   Upright Gobelin

Half of Front or Back   Half of Side Panel

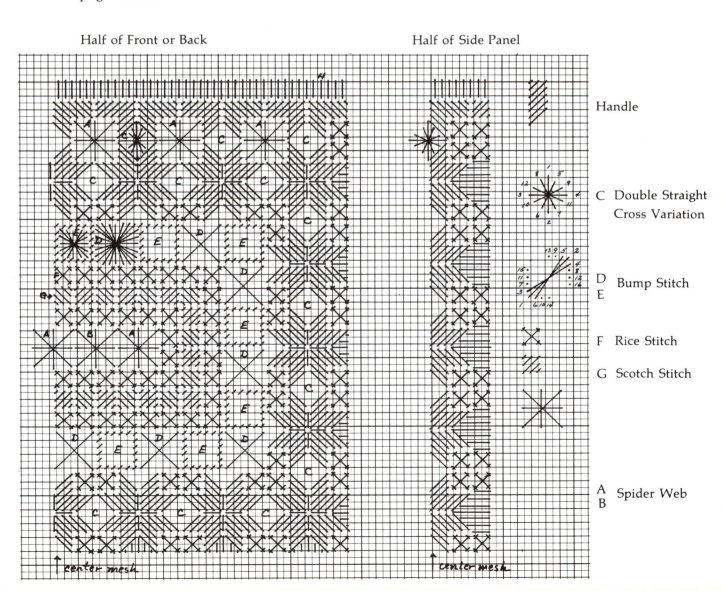

Handle

C Double Straight
   Cross Variation

D Bump Stitch
E

F Rice Stitch

G Scotch Stitch

A Spider Web
B

BARGELLO EYEGLASS CASE

Because they are small and quick to finish, designs for eyeglass cases can run the gamut from whimsical to traditional, dainty to outlandish, complicated to easy, bright to pale in color. This rather traditional example in a monochromatic rose color scheme is a de-sign of interlocking shieldlike shapes on #14 mono canvas. The generous size will accommodate the popular large size of many glasses. This is a gift you'll enjoy giving or keeping for yourself.

FINISHED SIZE
3¼ × 6 inches

MATERIALS
#14 white mono canvas, 10 × 10 inches
#20 tapestry needle
Persian yarn in 25-yard skeins as follows:
247, Clove Brown, 1 skein; 234, Toasty Pink,
    1 skein; 281, Antique Pink, 1 skein; 831,
    Pale Pink, 1 skein
Appropriate fabric for lining, approxi-
    mately 7½ × 7 inches

NOTE
Separate the yarn and work Bargello with
    two ply throughout.

INSTRUCTIONS
Tape the canvas and draw a vertical line
down the center to mark the fold line of the
case.

The chart details one half of either front or
back of the case. Start working at a point 2
inches from the bottom edge of the canvas
and 24 mesh to the right of the fold line. Beginning with stitch *a* count the row across to
the right to stitch *b*; then diagonally upward
to the left to stitch *c*, continuing again to the
right to stitch *d*. Fasten the yarn and attach
again at the bottom center next to stitch *a*.

Working left toward the fold line, repeat
the above in that direction to establish the
basic shield outline for half of the case.

Working as above, establish the brown
outlines in the other half of the case. Work
the remaining brown outlines in both sections. Fill in the motifs, following the chart
for color shading. Finish the top edge with a
row of Upright Gobelin Stitch as shown.
With a single strand of matching brown

yarn, work a row of Back Stitch between the
Gobelin row and the body of the case.

Block and finish the case according to the
instructions on page 156.

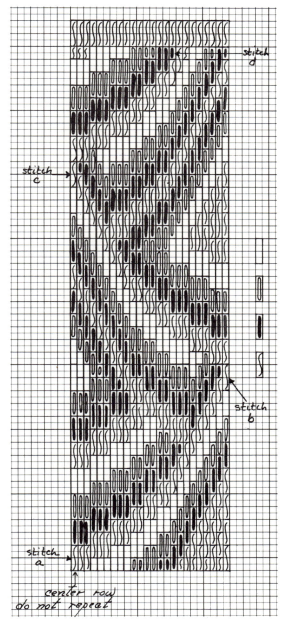

831 Pale Pink

281 Antique Pink

234 Toasty Pink

247 Clove Brown

58

BARGELLO IN A CONTEMPORARY MOOD

Part of Bargello's enduring appeal is certainly its ability to adapt to changing trends in fashion. Lipstick red, black, and white worked on a large mesh canvas transform this favorite old design into a striking pillow as modern as tomorrow. Its graphic detail and vivid color would fit naturally with the clean-lined sculptural furniture favored in many contemporary homes.

The interesting border effect evolved naturally when the spaces along the edges were filled in with solid color rather than maintaining the pattern to the sides. This idea works with many Bargello designs to produce pieces that have a more finished look.

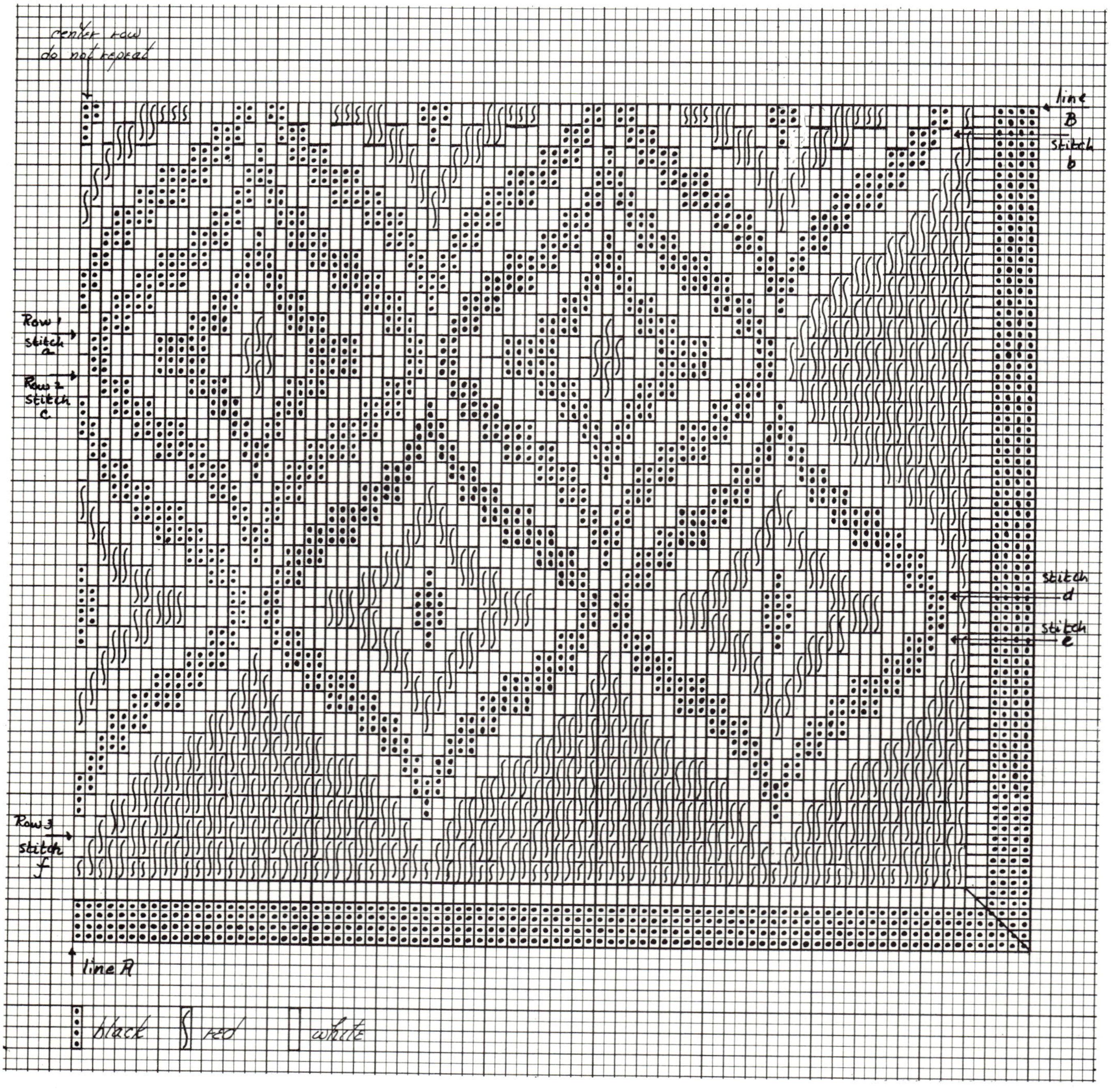
center row
do not repeat
line B
stitch b
Row 1 stitch a
Row 2 stitch c
stitch d
stitch e
Row 3 stitch f
line A
black
red
white

Finished size
13 × 14 inches

Materials
> #12 white mono canvas, approximately
> 17 × 18 inches
> #20 tapestry needle
> Persian yarn as follows: R-50, Dark Red,
> 50 yards; 005, White, 50 yards; 050,
> Black, 50 yards
> Appropriate fabric for pillow back, ½ yard

Note
Use the yarn full ply throughout as it comes
from the skein.

Instructions
Tape the canvas. Fold the canvas into quarters and mark the center. Draw a vertical and a horizontal line through the center point to divide the canvas into four quarters. These lines correspond to lines *A* and *B* marked on the chart. The chart represents one quarter of the pattern.

Begin working Row 1 with stitch *a* which is on line *A* (the vertical line) 24 mesh below the horizontal line *B*. Work across the row to stitch *b* and fasten the yarn. Attach the yarn again at stitch *a* and work to the left edge of the canvas ending again with stitch *b*. Attach the yarn at the center and work Row 2 from *c* to *d*; then repeat to the left for the remaining half of the row. Work Row 3 as indicated from stitch *e* at the right edge through *f* at the center of the canvas and continue across to the end at the left side with stitch *e*.

Turn the canvas and repeat these three rows to complete outlining the white motifs on the top section of the canvas.

Working out from the center of the canvas, fill in the outlined motifs, following the chart for color placement. At the outside edges fill in the curved spaces to form a straight edge, using solid red and maintaining the established stitching pattern.

Edge the piece with two rows of Upright Gobelin Stitch in black and white to form the border as shown. If you desire, work a row of Back Stitch with a single strand of matching yarn between the Gobelin rows.

Block and construct the pillow.

PASTEL BARGELLO PINCUSHION

Wouldn't it be more fun to give—or receive—this instead of a birthday card? The most delicate pastels, an easy Bargello design, and added touches of embroidery combine to make this a very feminine needlepoint sampler just the right size to finish into a pincushion. The mixture of techniques produces a texture and overall effect not possible when only one is used.

The view of the back of the pincushion shows the easy personalization that made this into a birthday special. Your own handwriting is the best for this kind of message, but if you worry that it is not fine enough, use one of the alphabets on pages 150, 152 and lay out your greeting on tracing paper. Make a transfer pattern and put it onto the fabric. Use either Back Stitch or Outline to embroider the letters.

FINISHED SIZE
4¾ × 5 inches

MATERIALS
#14 white mono canvas, 9 × 9 inches
#20 tapestry needle
Persian yarn as follows: 005, White, 6 yards; 458, Daffodil, 5 yards; 865, Powder Pink, 4 yards; 758, Light Summer Blue, 2 yards; 566, Iced Green, 1 yard
Appropriate fabric for back, 6 × 6 inches
Heavy white cotton lace about 2 inches wide, 1 yard
Small amount of fiberfilling

NOTE
Separate the yarn and work Bargello, needlepoint, and embroidery with two strands.

INSTRUCTIONS
After cutting and taping the canvas, start working by outlining the four blue Bargello circles. Next work the yellow rows inside the blue ones.

The slanted pink stitches that form the flowers should be placed as shown on the graph looking at the chart as if the lines were the threads of the canvas. (Each square petal is made up of seven slanted stitches crossing one, two, three, four, three, two, and one threads.)

After the pink flowers have been worked, fill in the remainder of the space inside the yellow rows (blue row in the center motif) with white Tent Stitch working as close to the Bargello as possible so no canvas shows. Use green to make Bullion Stitch leaves on top of the Tent Stitch. Lay center stitches over four threads, then place one stitch on each side, beginning and ending the stitches in the same mesh as the center stitch. The center of each flower is a yellow French Knot.

Work a row of Gobelin Stitch in pink with stitches worked over two threads around the entire square. Fill in the areas between the blue motif outlines and the pink border in white Bargello, following the stitching sequence established by the blue rows. Outline the entire square with a row of yellow Gobelin Stitch worked over four threads. If you desire, work a row of Back Stitch with a single strand of yellow between the pink and yellow borders.

If you decide to add a greeting on the back, plan the lettering and embroider it. Block and finish as a pincushion.

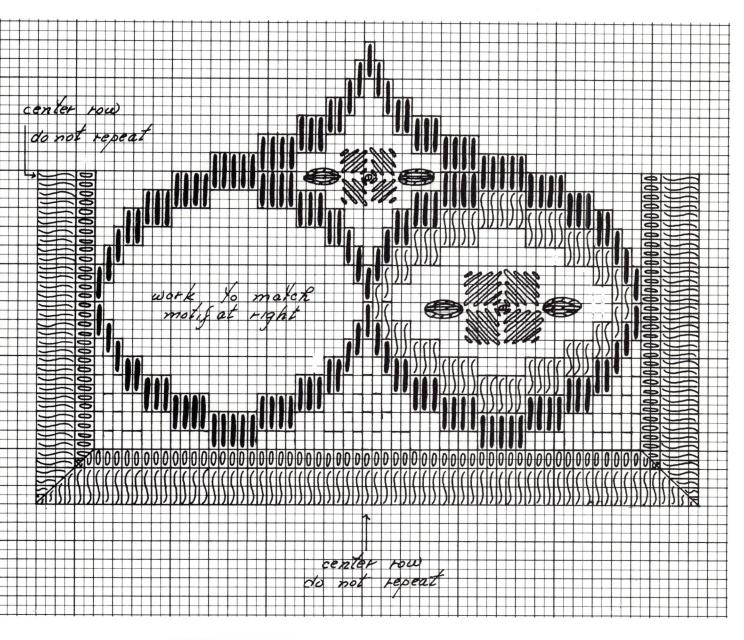

center row
do not repeat

work to match
motif at right

center row
do not repeat

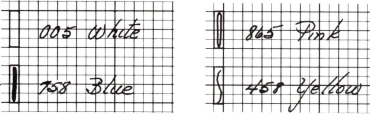

| | 005 White | | 865 Pink |
| | 758 Blue | | 458 Yellow |

ROMAN STRIPE THREE-PIECE SET

It's easy to become so involved in making large and technically complicated projects that one forgets the pleasure to be derived from gay little "fun" things like this set of bright accessories. It would be difficult to find a pattern much easier than the classic chevron used for all these pieces, and this is an obvious way to use some of those odds and ends of yarn we all accumulate. The finished articles shown use only eight colors in a regular repeat, but they would be very attractive worked in many shades randomly repeated.

This would be a good birthday or graduation gift. As shown, both sides of the key tag are worked in the Bargello pattern, but you can work the back in needlepoint and use the recipient's initials to make this a truly personal gift.

To enlarge any of the three pieces, either work on a larger mesh canvas or work a larger chevron pattern for each repeat.

FINISHED SIZE

Glasses case—2½ × 5¾ inches

Key tag—2½ × 3½ inches

Hatband—1 × 22 inches

MATERIALS

#17 cream mono canvas as follows—for glasses case, one piece 9 × 9 inches; for key tag, one piece 9 × 10 inches; for hatband, one piece 2 × 24 inches

#22 tapestry needle

Persian yarn as follows: Approximately 10 yards of each of the following colors or an assortment of odds and ends—050, Black; R-60, Medium Dark Red; R-70, Frosted Cherry; 975, Pumpkin Seed; 456, Baby Yellow; 723, Bright Blue; 773, Teal Blue; 524, Dark Green

Appropriate fabric 9 × 9 inches for glasses case lining; small amount of fiber filling for key tag; ¾ yard ribbon for hatband lining

NOTE

Separate the yarn and work with two ply throughout.

INSTRUCTIONS

Glasses Case: Tape the canvas edges and draw a line down the middle to mark the fold line of the case.

The diagram shows one entire side—either front or back—of the key tag. The glasses case is an elongated version of the tag. Work one chevron panel in its entirety before starting the next.

Begin Section 1 with Row 1 at a point 2 inches down from the top of the canvas and four mesh to the right of the fold line. Work down using the colors in order until Row 8 has been completed. Repeat Rows 1 through 8 once more. Fill in the triangle at the top to form a straight edge with green as shown on the chart. Fill in the two triangles at the bottom with black (see photograph).

Work the row of Gobelin stitches separating Sections 1 and 2. Begin Section 2 at the bottom and work upward to reverse both the chevron and the color order. Outline the completed two sections with black Gobelin border as shown on the chart.

Work back to match front, placing the adjoining Gobelin border on the fold line.

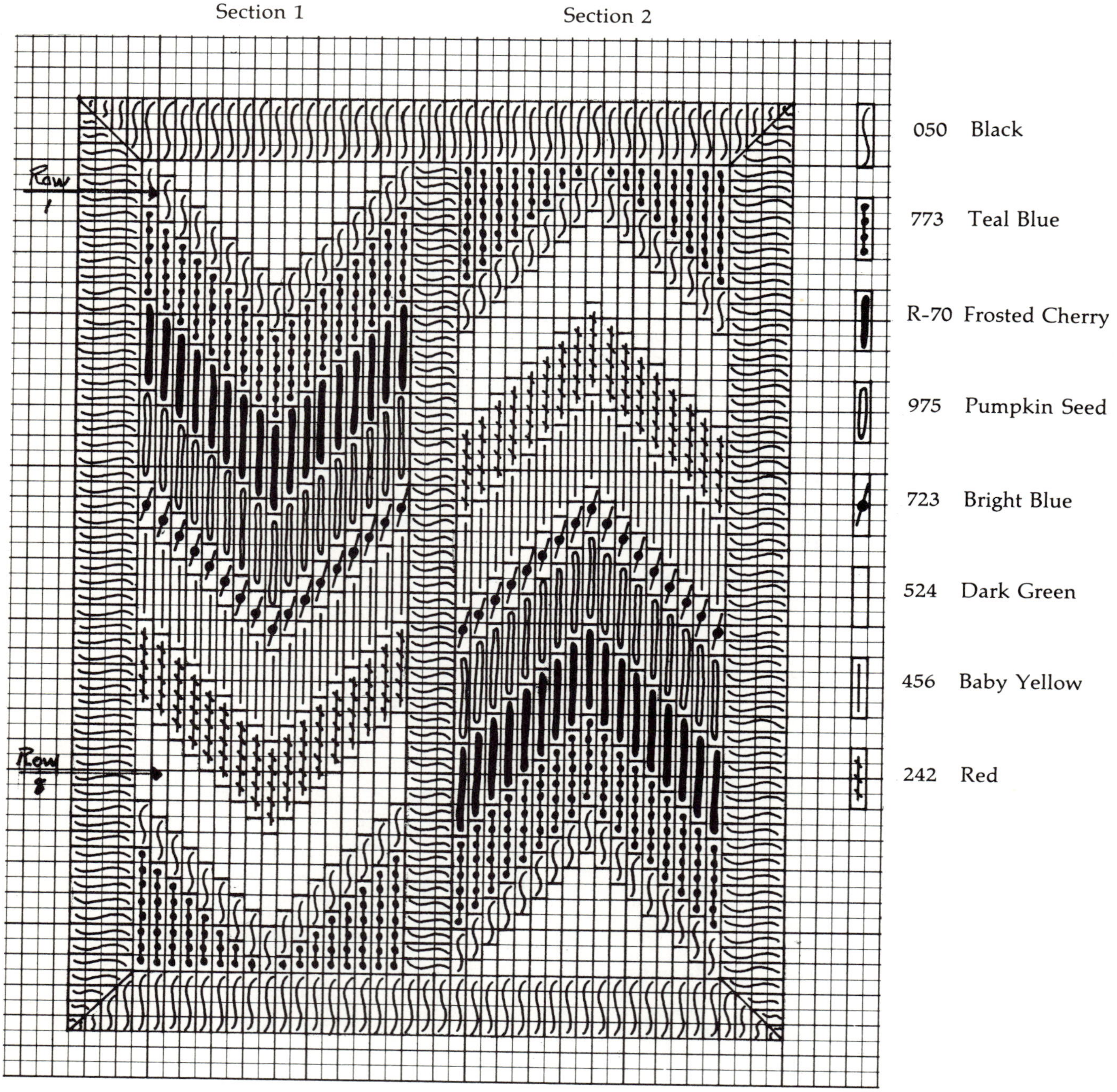
Section 1
Section 2
Row 1
Row 8
050 Black
773 Teal Blue
R-70 Frosted Cherry
975 Pumpkin Seed
723 Bright Blue
524 Dark Green
456 Baby Yellow
242 Red

Block and construct the case following the instructions on page 156.

Key Tag: Tape the canvas and draw a vertical line down the center to mark the fold line of the tag.

The chart shows the front or back of the tag in its entirety. Begin working Section 1 with Row 1, 2 inches down from the top of the canvas and four mesh to the right of the fold line. Work Section 1 completely; follow with the Gobelin row, separating the sections; complete Section 2; then outline with black Gobelin Stitch as shown.

Work back to match completed front, placing the adjoining Gobelin border on the fold line. An optional finish would be to use the recipient's initials and work the back entirely in Tent Stitch to make a really personal gift.

Block. Trim canvas borders to ½ inch and press to wrong side, mitering the corners. Fold tag in half on fold line, and whip the edges together with black yarn leaving a small opening to receive the stuffing material. Place a little bit of polyester fiber filling inside and close the opening. Attach a key ring to one corner.

Hatband: The hatband is a linear repeat of Rows 1 through 8 for the length necessary to reach around the crown of a hat. Finish one end in a point following the line of the chevron and the other with a straight edge. Work a row of black Gobelin Stitch border with stitches three threads long around entire piece. Block. Trim canvas borders to ½ inch and press to wrong side. Whip ribbon to back as a lining. Ends of band may be whipped together and band slipped down over crown, or a Velcro fastener can be attached to make changing bands easy.

CARNATION PILLOW

The museum's tag on the fragment indicated the piece was American Eighteenth Century and had probably been a chair seat. Not much remained and the fragile piece was in bad condition, but there were my favorite carnations and those wonderful colors of the period. The foundation material was not canvas as we know it but a loosely woven linen with a thread count of 24 or 28 to the inch on which it must have been extremely difficult to work a counted embroidery. Most of the yarn was wool, but some of the golds were silk, some cotton. The background was a marvelous Turkey red, the carnations alternately blue and gold.

Counting out the pattern to chart it was an exercise in patience for the limp piece was completely out of shape. The challenge was complicated by the fact that no two flowers were exactly alike although at a glance they seemed so because of the fine thread count of the background.

Finally several flowers were charted and the carnation shown and repeated here is one of them. The canvas for this pillow is 17 to the inch to allow for pretty shading within the flowers, to keep them fairly small, and to retain some of the flavor of the old piece. Bargello works up so quickly that using the fine canvas does not make the project one that takes a prohibitively long time.

This pillow, made as a Christmas gift, is personalized in the spaces outlined by the two partial carnations at the bottom. The outline of the top of the flower was counted onto the canvas, the lettering added (for Pat in one space, Margaret in the other); then as much of the Bargello pattern as would fit was worked. Finally the rest of the space was filled with Tent Stitch in gold. When the pillow is stuffed and sitting on a chair, the lettering does not show, but it remains for Pat to enjoy.

FINISHED SIZE
11 × 11 inches

MATERIALS
#17 cream-colored mono canvas, 15 × 15 inches
Persian yarn as follows: 438, Buttercup, 16 yards; 467, Light Medium Yellow, 25 yards; 457, Canary Yellow, 35 yards; 447, Mustard, 28 yards; 427, Medium Gold, 15 yards; 570, Celery Leaf, 7 yards; 555, Green Giant, 6 yards; 510, Medium Green, 7 yards; 843, Fire Ball, 6 yards; 365, French Navy, 45 yards
#22 tapestry needle
Fabric for pillow back, approximately ½ yard

NOTE
Separate the yarn and work the Bargello stitches with two ply.

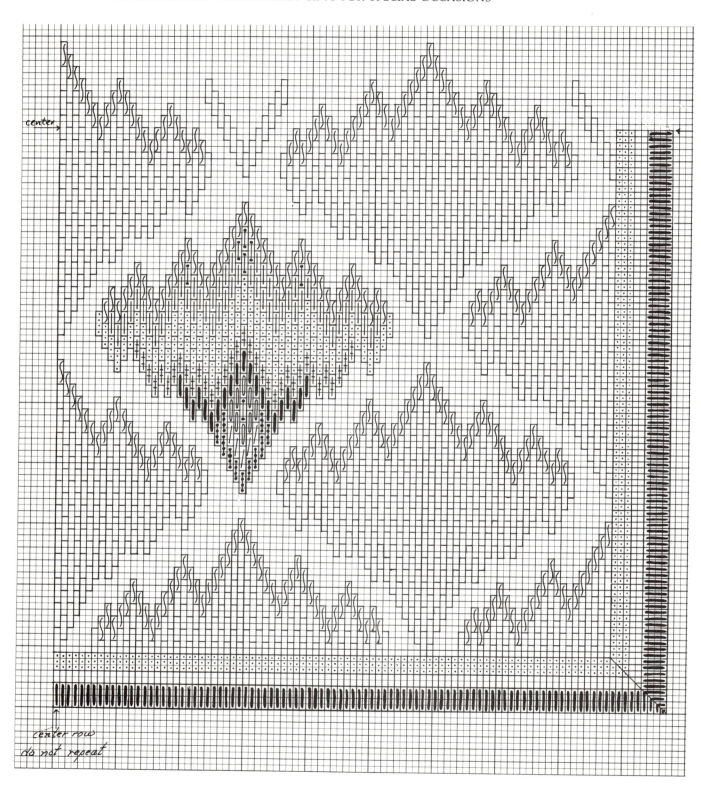

center

center row
do not repeat

INSTRUCTIONS

The chart shows one quarter of the pillow plus the small portions of motifs that overlap into the upper adjoining section. The boundaries of the quarter are indicated by the end of border charting and the arrows marking the center mesh. Note that the design is not exactly square; it is off by several mesh to allow full carnations to be repeated top to bottom and for the full half to be repeated at the side edges. The fraction of an inch difference is not apparent in the finished pillow, but the incomplete carnations would be a distraction.

All carnations are to be worked exactly alike. All those that make up one quarter of the design are laid out on the chart to show their placement. Only one is completely keyed to show the color placement.

Although background stitches are not indicated, they are to be worked in blue Brick Stitch, following the outlines of the carnations. The flowers are spaced so the Brick pattern fits perfectly around them. Partial stitches are necessary only at the side border edges to make a straight line.

Fold the canvas and mark the center. This corresponds to the canvas center marked on the chart. Count up from that point and with 438 begin working the carnation as charted. As soon as the row of 438 is placed, switch to the fully charted carnation and work from it.

Work in the order you find most convenient. You may want to finish each flower before starting the next, or you may prefer to work on three or four at a time, working all of one color in each so there is not so much changing needle and thread. I prefer the latter and I also start working background around completed flowers to avoid having to do it all at the end.

To finish the pillow, work the three rows of Upright Gobelin Stitch border, mitering the corners as shown on the chart. If little specks of canvas show in the border, work a row of Back Stitch with a single strand of matching yarn in the space between the rows. This is a pretty finish which gives the rows a very defined outline and covers the specks of canvas at the same time.

This allover pattern is a very good one to use for chair seats or upholstery, and it fits well into either an Early American or a contemporary decorating scheme.

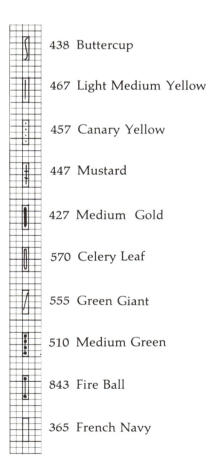

438 Buttercup

467 Light Medium Yellow

457 Canary Yellow

447 Mustard

427 Medium Gold

570 Celery Leaf

555 Green Giant

510 Medium Green

843 Fire Ball

365 French Navy

Embroidery on Fabric

Since most needleworkers are versatile and work in many mediums, this collection of gifts includes the spectrum of the most preferred kinds of embroidery today. It includes traditional needlepoint and crewel, embroidery with lustrous cotton threads, Bargello, fancy canvas stitches on plastic mesh and Counted Cross Stitch. The objects divide into two basic categories: those worked on a canvas foundation and those worked on a fabric background.

To make possible the duplication of the projects in this book, each has been presented as a finished, photographed model, with a complete list of the materials needed, detailed working instructions, and either a full-sized drawing or a graph with the needed stitch and color notations. Individual pieces may be reproduced exactly like the original, or personal changes in colors, fabric, or stitches can be made with only a small adjustment in the kinds and quantities of materials needed.

MATERIALS

FABRICS

Each project begins with a list of the materials used for the finished model shown. Note that the fabric dimensions are usually given in the exact size needed rather than in approximate yards. These measurements allow for borders and seam allowances and are supplied to make the use of small pieces of fabric already on hand. Obviously some of these fabric pieces are very small—as in the 6-inch square for a pincushion—so it will be necessary to sew on side and end extensions of muslin or other scrap fabric in order to put the piece in a frame or hoop. If you have enough material leave the piece larger, but if you have only a scrap, use it by adding extensions!

The fabrics used for these projects are all easily obtained modern materials found in most needlework shops or department stores. Linen is a favorite background as it is easy to work on and wears very well. There is a variety of colors available and a number of weaves and weights as well. The kind used is specified in the instructions when it is crucial to the look of the finished piece. When unbleached muslin is used, it should be the best quality and firmest weave that can be found. When Hardanger fabric is required, the thread count and color are specified to ensure that the finished piece has the same appearance and size as the original.

As a general rule buy the best fabric available. Good quality is the best investment you can make in needlework materials as the embroidery is easier and the final project much more valuable. When you consider the time and talent you put into any embroidery project, it is easy to see how unwise it is to lavish so much on unworthy materials.

Another consideration when buying fabric for an embroidery project is the final use of the piece. Obviously, a chair seat or upholstered item should be made of long-wearing material that will not have to be replaced in a short time. A pillow or picture can be made of less substantial fabric as long as the quality is worthy of the embroidery. Some of the new easy-care fabrics have been treated with chemicals and heat which drastically shorten the life of the material. Think about all these things when selecting the foundation for your work.

YARNS AND EMBROIDERY THREADS

Persian-type Yarns: The wool Persian-type yarns used in the projects in this book are all Columbia-Minerva Needlepoint and Crewel Yarn, and the color numbers that appear in the instructions are for that yarn. It is available in both 10- and 25-yard skeins in an enticing array of colors. This yarn works very well, makes lovely soft stitches, does not wear thin if proper length is used, is colorfast, and its 100 percent wool fiber content makes it long wearing and practical. The three-ply strand is convenient as the yarn can be used for heavy work as it is or separated to be used for finer stitches. A note at the beginning of each set of instructions indicates the number of strands of yarn to be used for that particular project.

Other brands of yarn of equal quality can be substituted in any of the instructions as long as the yarn is of similar weight and appropriate construction. To make the substitution of other yarns possible, yarn quantities for each project are given in yards rather than in skeins. These quantities apply to three-ply strands regardless of the number of strands with which the stitches are to be worked. This more accurate forecasting of needed yarn also makes possible the use of small amounts of yarn that may already be on hand.

Cotton Embroidery Floss: Any good reliable brand of cotton embroidery floss can be used for the projects that use that thread. Most of these are soft, lustrous and easy to use. Most have only color numbers for identification so the descriptive names in the instructions are added to help in substitution of other brands of floss. Most are packed in convenient 8-yard skeins and are the standard six-ply strand. A note in the instructions indicates the number of strands to be used in each kind of stitch in the project. If a specific brand of floss was used in a project and it is important that the colors be true to the original, the brand name is given so either that brand or a substitute in comparable colors can be used.

Yarn and Embroidery Thread Requirements: The yardage suggested for each project is based on that used to finish the model shown. There is a great variation in the way people work—some tend to work loosely, some are very careful and sparing, while others apply yarn heavily—and this has been taken into consideration. The yardage specified should be enough for the average careful worker to complete the piece with a small, unavoidable surplus. If you know you are extravagant with yarn or if you intend to change stitches or enlarge the piece, you will want to buy extra yarn to avoid running short in the middle of the work.

NEEDLES

Choose embroidery needles carefully. They should be the familiar long-eyed crewel type, and the size should be suitable for both the fabric and the yarn to be used. Ideally, the needle should pierce the fabric easily, making an opening just large enough for the yarn to pass through without excessive friction.

Find the best quality needles available, as less expensive ones corrode quickly and are difficult to use.

THIMBLE

Use a thimble if you are in the habit of using it for other sewing, but do not fret if you find it is more trouble than it is worth. Beautiful embroidery can be worked with or without a thimble, and it is purely a matter of personal preference.

SCISSORS

Good embroidery scissors are an essential part of every embroiderer's equipment, and they should be used for embroidery only. Find a small 3- to 4-inch pair with tapered blades that are sharp to the very tips. Keep them in a case to protect both the blades and your embroidery.

TRANSFER PENCILS

Transfer or copy pencils make the job of putting the design on the fabric an easy task. Available in most needlework shops at a very nominal cost, the pencils are made in magenta, yellow, and blue.

These pencils replace dressmaker carbon, pouncing, and all the other old methods for transferring designs to fabric. The lines created by the pencils are clear and fairly permanent. Most will not rub off while the embroidery is being worked. Some wash out more easily than others, but those that do not come off with soap and water can usually be removed with ordinary household cleaning fluid.

TRACING PAPER

Since you will be tracing the designs and using the same tracing for the transfer pattern, it is usually best to use a fairly heavy paper like that found in pads in art supply stores. Most of these will stand up to the heat of the iron and provide enough protection for the fabric to prevent scorching.

HOOPS AND FRAMES

It is best to work crewel and other embroideries on fabric stretched in a hoop or frame. Learning to work with one hand above and one hand under the work requires a little adjustment, but with a little practice, it becomes automatic, and the stitching is very fast, the stitches are beautiful and there is never any bunching from too-tight tension.

There are many styles of hoops and frames: hand-held, freestanding, roller-type and artists' stretcher frames. All are satisfactory and the choice should be made according to the project at hand and your own personal preference.

TRANSFERRING DESIGNS TO FABRIC

Line drawings of the exact size of the finished embroideries are provided so there will be no enlarging problems for those who cannot draw. The new transfer pencils make it possible to put one of the designs onto fabric ready to be worked by simply making a tracing of the design, going over the tracing with the transfer pencil, and then ironing the pattern onto the fabric.

Large designs have been divided into sections and may be on as many as four pages. All sections have slashed dividing lines and are labeled: Upper Right Section, Lower Right Section, to assist in proper copying of the designs. Also, a portion of the design from the adjoining section is always shown

and these should match when the tracing is done.

To copy a design that has been divided into four quarters and is shown on four pages, fold a large piece of tracing paper into quarters. Open it flat and place it over one of the sections matching the fold lines of the paper to the slashed lines on the drawing. Lightly trace the portion of design shown, including the parts that overlap into the next sections. (Trace lightly so the book is not marred by impressions left by the pencil.) Move the tracing paper to the next section, match the fold lines to the slashed lines on the drawing, and the portions of this section that have already been traced will match the drawing. Trace the remainder of that section. Repeat to complete the design.

Check full-size tracing and make certain that lines which run from one section to the next are smooth and the pattern is perfect. Turn the tracing over, and with a sharp copy pencil go over all the design areas to make a transfer pattern. Work with a very sharp pencil to keep the lines fine because they spread with the heat of the iron. If you make a mistake, begin again with a new sheet of paper (just place another sheet of tracing paper over the first), since the error will transfer to the fabric and may not be in an area that will be covered over with embroidery.

Make a small sample transfer and test it on a scrap of the material or a corner of the actual piece to check the iron temperature as well as the visibility of the color of the pencil on the fabric. If fairly heavy parchment is used for the tracing paper, the heat of the iron should not scorch the fabric. If the fabric being used is delicate or the sample tested shows a danger of scorching, add an extra layer of paper over the transfer to protect the fabric.

Placing the transfer-pencil-side down, center the pattern on the fabric and carefully iron until the design transfers to the fabric. Move the iron over the paper carefully to avoid displacing it or smearing the lines.

The embroidery should be worked to completely cover the transfer lines, but when the work is finished, if some traces of lines are still visible, washing with mild soap will usually remove them. Try washing the test sample. If it does not wash clean, try moistening the area with cleaning fluid and then washing to remove odor.

IDENTIFICATION OF YARNS AND STITCHES ON THE CHARTS

Capital letters on the chart indicate the stitches that were used on the model, while the numbers identify the color or colors of yarn. The color numbers are the manufacturer's numbers and the identifying color names are also included alongside each chart.

Wear and tear on the book can be reduced if you make photocopies of the charts and use them as working guides instead of carrying around the bulky book. Also, if color substitutions have been made, note them on the copy for handy reference.

In some areas of design several color numbers appear. This usually denotes that the area is to be worked in the stitch indicated and shaded in the colors noted in the order in which they appear on the drawing. This is explained in the instructions of each particu-

lar piece to make these subtle colorings clear.

Sometimes in very small motifs or in places where there are a number of identical motifs all to be worked in the same color and stitch, only one or two will be keyed and arrows will point to only one or two. This indicates that all are to be worked alike.

THE INSTRUCTIONS

The book is written cookbook-style—each project gives a list of materials needed, the chart or design, and a set of detailed instructions. If the suggested "ingredients" are used and the instructions followed, the results should be a good duplication of the original pictured item.

Read through the written working instructions before beginning to work. These are as detailed as each piece seemed to indicate and reflect my own working methods. A sincere effort has been made to make them easy to follow and to provide all the information needed. If a particular working order is included in the instructions, it indicates that experimentation has shown that it is usually the easiest method, but your own personal way may be faster for you. My tricks may help you; yours could easily be better for you, so after reading mine, you make the decision.

One of the biggest advantages in working from a book rather than from a prepared kit is that it is possible to make changes and personalize the finished product. If you do make changes, be careful to take these into consideration when purchasing materials. Naturally a simple color change will not require extra yarn, but a change in size or stitches may.

READY TO EMBROIDER

Prevent Fraying of the Edges of the Fabric

It is a good idea to put a row of zigzag machine stitching or a narrow single fold hem around the edges of fabric to keep it from fraying as you work. Masking tape is good for canvas but not desirable on fabrics. Transparent tape is unsatisfactory—messy, sticky and non-adherent.

Working in a Hoop or Frame

Except for Cross Stitch, most embroideries are easier and the stitches faster and more even when the background fabric is stretched tightly in a frame or hoop. Most round hoops have a working area that is smaller than that to be embroidered, with the result that the piece will have to be moved one or more times to be completed. Most stitches are firm enough not to be damaged or stretched if the hoop is fastened on them, but it is always a good idea to remove the hoop when the embroidery is put away between work sessions. If the piece is being worked on a stretcher frame and is stretched very tightly, release the tension on the fabric slightly when you put the work away.

Working on a hoop or frame ensures even stitching, avoids puckering, and generally produces better embroidery. Some embroidery stitches can be worked neatly without the support of a frame—indeed some teachers recommend that these stitches be learned without it—but others must have the firm, taut background provided by the frame. For this reason, it is simplest to learn to work them all on the frame rather than try to juggle the two methods.

Learning to embroider with one hand above and one below the hoop does take some small adjustment, but once the technique is mastered, the stitching becomes easier and progresses rapidly. Most people prefer to have the right hand under the hoop and the left on top to return the needle, but there is no reason this cannot be reversed if it is more comfortable.

Adding Muslin Extensions to Small Pieces

If the piece of fabric for your project is too small to fit into your favorite hoop, enlarge it by simply sewing muslin—or other scrap fabric—to the four sides. I just overlap the two fabrics in a flat seam and run a row of zigzag stitching close to the edge of the smaller piece. The seam is not bulky and makes it easy to snip off the extension when the work is finished.

Length of Strand of Yarn

Work with short threads. Normally 12 inches to 15 inches is sufficient. If wool is being used, long strands will wear thin and not cover transfer lines well. If cotton floss is being used, a long strand may twist and knot, the individual strands may separate, and the long length is very awkward.

If wool wears thin even when a short length is being used, check the needle. It may be a size too small, causing too much wear on the yarn as it is being pulled through the fabric. Also, some needles have eyes shaped in such a way that they cut the yarn if too much pulling takes place. Keep an assortment of good needles on hand and try several until you find the right one.

WORKING WITH THE TWIST OF THE YARN

Each strand of wool yarn is made up of hundreds of short fibers spun into a continuous thread. If you pull the strand between your thumb and forefinger, you can feel the grain or spinning direction. Pulled in one direction the thread feels smooth, while the shorter fiber ends can be felt if the direction is reversed. The yarn should be threaded into the needle so the smooth side follows the needle into the fabric. This reduces abrasion and wear on the yarn and produces smoother embroidery.

THREADING THE NEEDLE

Never wet or twist yarn in order to thread the needle. There are three easy ways, one of which will work for you.

Fold method: Hold the needle between your thumb and forefinger with the eye facing you. Loop the yarn end around the needle and pull it tightly to form a fold. Holding the fold tightly, gently withdraw the needle. Still holding the fold tightly, force it through the eye of the needle.

Squeeze method: Press the end of the yarn tightly between the thumb and forefinger of one hand. With the other hand, force the eye of the needle over the tightly held yarn. With only a little practice, you will be able to fit the yarn right into the eye of the needle.

Paper method: Cut a piece of paper about an inch long and narrow enough to fit through the eye of the needle. Fold the paper in half and place the cut end of the yarn in the folded paper. Pass the folded end of the paper through the eye of the needle and the yarn will easily pass through.

You can also buy a little wire needle threader and keep it in your work basket if you prefer.

EMBROIDER WITHOUT KNOTS

Learn to embroider without knots. This is not the impossible task it may seem at first. Begin stitching on the right side with several small Running or Back Stitches in an area that will be covered with embroidery. Leave the end on the right side and cut it off when the area is reached. Fasten the end of a strand in the same manner. This method avoids knots, saves the time that would be spent turning over the frame to fasten ends, and eliminates loose ends hanging on the back. The ends can also be utilized as extra padding in stitches like Satin by holding them in place and working over them.

COVERING THE TRANSFER LINES

Embroider slightly beyond the outlines of the design on the fabric to be certain the color from the transfer pencil is hidden. If wool yarn is being used, the stitches should be loose enough to allow the yarn to relax and provide good coverage.

COUNTED CROSS STITCH

Counted Cross Stitch is an engrossing embroidery that has a beautiful and nostalgic appeal. Worked on an even-weave fabric, the stitches are identical in size and always in perfect alignment. The embroidery is so much more beautiful than that worked on stamped crosses that it is impossible to accept the irregularity of the stamped work after Counted Cross is tried.

Choose good quality Hardanger fabric with a thread count as specified in the instructions to ensure that the piece will be the same size as the one pictured. To cut perfectly straight, pull a thread and cut on the line that results.

The top stitch of every Cross Stitch must always slant in one direction throughout an entire piece of embroidery to assure a smooth, regular appearance. To avoid confusion about the slant of the stitches, always hold the piece in the same position. If it has selvages use them as the guide, always working on the piece with the selvages running the same way.

When working from the Counted Cross Stitch charts and using Hardanger fabric, note that each square represents a stitch of a particular color worked over a prescribed number of threads. The pieces in this book are all on Hardanger fabric, and the stitches are all worked over a square of two vertical and two horizontal threads. When counting the unworked spaces between motifs, be sure to allow for this.

Work complete individual motifs rather than attempting to work across an entire row. Do not "jump" across unworked background spaces with long threads. Dark threads show through the fabric when the piece is stretched, and the threads pulled too tightly will prevent the piece from being blocked flat.

Two basting threads through the center of the piece—one horizontally and one vertically—are great time savers and help in the counting for placement of motifs. It is usually best to find an anchor point from which to start counting and work outward from that pont. Some prefer to start working at the exact center of a piece, while others prefer to begin at the top corner and proceed downward. Your method should be based on individual working preferences as well as on the design itself. Either method works perfectly if it is carried through to the finish.

The charts for the larger pieces in this book have been divided onto several pages. Note that slashed lines mark the center rows of these pieces and that they appear on all sections to help orient one to the other. These lines also correspond to the bastings through the center of the fabric. Individual motifs that cross from one section to the adjacent one are shown in full on both charts, also to help orient one to the other. When only half of a piece is shown, it is understood that the other side is worked from the same chart, counting stitches in the opposite direction.

Counted Cross can be worked with or without a hoop. Very fine work in which the stitches are worked over single threads with one strand of floss—and which is not used in the projects in this book—are generally easier to handle if they are placed in a hoop. Some even-weave linens are best worked in a hoop, but for the most part a hoop is not really necessary.

THE SURFACE STITCHES

Embroidery stitches are many and fascinating. There are hundreds of them and hundreds of variations. The study of the stitches—the romance and history surrounding them, their geographic development and distribution, their colorful and often intriguing names, the intricacies of working methods—is an absorbing hobby. It is an investigation that can carry you to the farthest reaches of the globe or one that you can research in museums, libraries, and antique galleries. It can be as simple as experimenting with needle, fabric and a book, or as expensive and adventuresome as a world tour. Every needleworker gets caught up in it sooner or later and usually adds a great deal of enjoyment to embroidery as a result of the experience. The stitches that follow are few in number—only the ones used in the production of the projects in the book—but coincidentally perhaps the best and most useful of the general embroidery stitches. These are the basics which form the nucleus of a good stitch vocabulary, and they can be combined in innumerable ways to create interesting embroidery.

Instead of the familiar line drawings to show stitch construction, the stitches are shown photographically as they are being worked. Each photograph shows a few completed stitches, the needle inserted as if to continue, with the thread always in the proper position. The result is clear, almost graphic in detail. It is like having a teacher right there to demonstrate a stitch.

To learn a new stitch, prepare the fabric in a frame or hoop, thread the needle, read the instructions for the stitch and examine the photograph. Next, actually work the stitch, carefully following the written instructions step by step. Check the work with the completed stitches shown on the photograph to make sure they have been worked correctly. The combination of written and pictorial instructions makes it possible to learn new stitches effortlessly.

Often the written stitch directions give hints about how a stitch can be used most effectively. It may be helpful to know that a particular stitch is very good as an outline but can also be worked in close rows to fill a space entirely. Other little remarks found in the instructions are aimed at helping the reader to use the stitches in a variety of ways.

Although the instructions for the projects list exactly which stitches were used for the pictured model, feel free to experiment with others and thus personalize the designs. Have a little extra yarn on hand if you do this because the substituted stitches may use more yardage, and you will undoubtedly do a little ripping in the beginning. This experimentation is not possible with a kit because the yarns are limited, but it is a feature of working from a book that should definitely be used to best advantage. Your finished pieces will not be exactly like the pictured models, but they will be partly your own creation, and for this reason they will give you additional pleasure.

BACK STITCH

An easy outline stitch, Back Stitch makes a neat line that resembles a row of machine stitches. It may be used as an outline or can be worked in closely spaced rows to fill a large area. Worked very small, it is an ideal stitch for lettering and curved lines.

To begin a row of stitches: Bring the needle to the surface at *A*, which is one stitch length from the beginning of the row, and pull the thread through. Go down at *B* and back to the surface at *C* keeping the distance from *A* to *B* and *A* to *C* equal. Pull the yarn through to form a stitch. Insert the needle again at *A* and continue stitching, keeping the stitch length as uniform as possible.

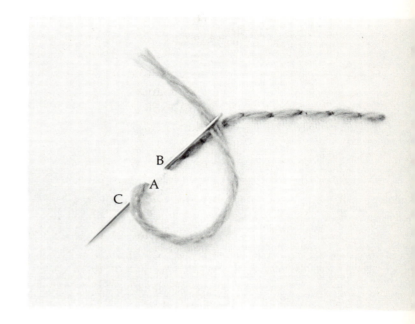

BULLION KNOT

The Bullion Knot's coiled length makes an interesting raised flower center or detail in many different situations. It can be made to lie flat along a line, or to curve, or to form a rosebudlike cluster.

To begin: Bring the needle up at *A* and pull the yarn through. Go down at *B* and come up again at *A* but do not pull the yarn through. Wrap the yarn around the needle until the length of the coil is roughly the distance from *A* to *B*.

Hold the wrap firmly and work the needle through the coil of yarn. Continuing to hold the wrap, pull the yarn all the way through so the stitch lies flat on the fabric. Take the needle to the wrong side at *B*.

If the yarn is wrapped around the needle so the coil is the same length as the distance from *A* to *B*, the stitch will lie flat on the fab-

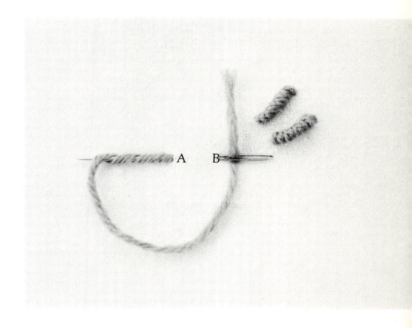

ric. To make a curved stitch, wrap the yarn around the needle a few extra times and proceed as for a flat stitch.

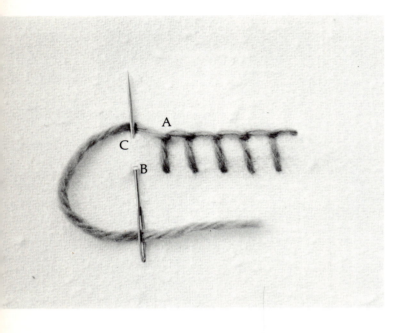

BUTTONHOLE STITCH

Sometimes called the Blanket Stitch, Button-hole can be worked with the loops spaced widely and evenly as shown in the photograph, or in many variations that group the stitches in decorative patterns. When the stitches are placed close together, they become an effective filling stitch with a slightly raised edge.

To work: Bring the needle up at *A* and pull the yarn through. Holding the yarn above the needle to form a loop, insert the needle into the fabric at *B* and bring it back to the surface at *C*. Pull the needle through, adjusting the tension of the loop to allow the stitch to lie flat. Continue in this manner.

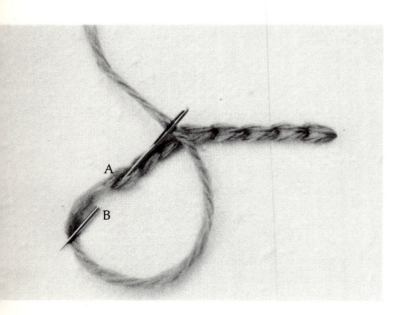

CHAIN STITCH

A single row of Chain Stitch forms a broad outline, while closely spaced rows following the form of a motif make an effective filling stitch.

To start: Bring the needle up at *A* pulling the yarn through. Holding the thread below the needle to form a loop, insert the needle again at *A* and bring the needle up at *B*. Pull the yarn through and adjust the loop.

When working the rows as a filling, begin by outlining the outside edge of the motif and then work concentric rows toward the center, maintaining the same direction for all rows and allowing the rows to flow in the same lines as the shape being filled. In the center, fill any small section that will not accommodate full rows with the portions of rows that fit.

CROSS STITCH

Equally at home on canvas or fabric, the Cross Stitch is very easy but nonetheless beautiful and effective. The secret of perfect Cross Stitch is always to have the base stitches slanting in one direction throughout the piece. When making multiple stitches in one color, it is best to work across making all the base stitches (shown by the slanting stitch A to B on the photograph) and then return, placing the second stitches on top as shown. Single stitches should be completed individually.

To work a row of stitches: Bring the needle to the surface at A and pull the yarn through. Insert the needle at B and bring it up again at C which is directly below B and to the right on the same line as A. Pull the yarn through to form the slanted stitch. Continue to the end of the row. Return by working as shown by the needle, inserting it and bringing it to the surface in the same holes made by the previous stitches.

FISHBONE STITCH

The Fishbone Stitch is ideal filling for many leaf forms and is thus a very much used crewel stitch. It can be worked solid (as in the photograph) or with the stitches widely spaced for an open look. The first stitch should be fairly long to ensure that the side stitches lie on a good slant.

To begin: Bring the needle up at A, pull the yarn through and go down at B which is about ¼ inch down the center line from A. Come up at C which is to the left and very slightly below A on the outline. Holding the thread below the needle to form a loop, go down at D, which corresponds to C but is to

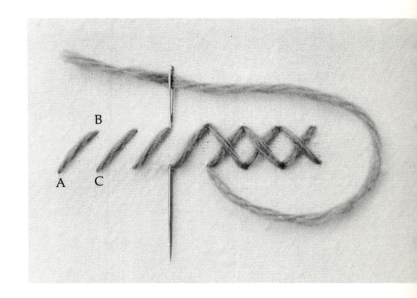

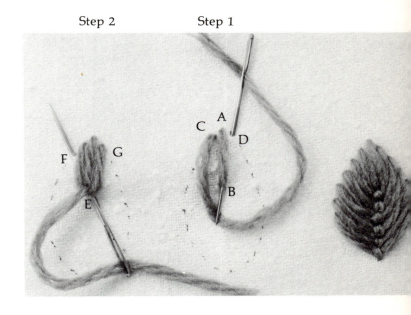

Step 2   Step 1

the right of *A*. Bring the needle to the surface again at *B* and pull the yarn through, adjusting the loop so the stitch lies flat (end of Step 1 in photograph).

Make a small stitch across the loop by inserting the needle at *E* as shown in Step 2. Come up at *F* on the left side and repeat the loop-forming and tie-down stitch until the area is covered.

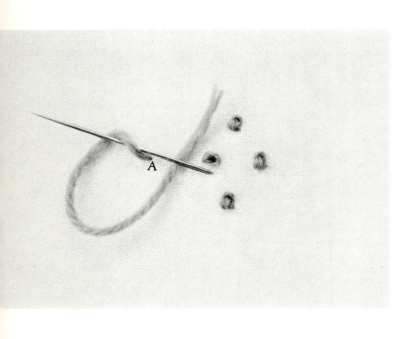

FRENCH KNOT

French Knots can be used as seeding, packed together to make solid textured areas, worked in rows of shaded colors, or grouped to make interesting flower centers and other details.

To make the knot: Bring the needle to the surface at *A* and pull the yarn through. Wrap the yarn around the needle once; then insert the tip of the needle into the fabric close to *A* but with at least one thread intervening. Pull the yarn to tighten the loop around the needle. Pull the needle through to the back of the work.

HERRINGBONE STITCH

Herringbone is good for wide lines, borders, and as a filling stitch. Work from left to right.

Begin at left by bringing the yarn to the surface at *A* and pulling it through. With the yarn in the position shown, insert the needle at *B* and bring it out at *C*. Pull it through. Throw the yarn to the top, insert the needle at *D*, and bring it to the surface at *E*. Repeat to complete row.

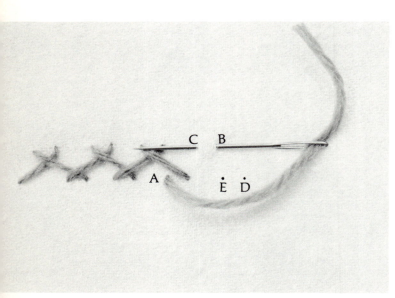

LONG AND SHORT STITCH

Long and Short produces shading and detail unequaled by any other. It may be worked in even rows or in an irregular pattern that causes a painted effect. The basic stitching foundation is the same for the two methods.

Only the first or outside row has both Long and Short Stitches, a quirk that is often confusing to the beginner. To practice this stitch, use a heavy yarn and work the rows in shades of one color, beginning with the darkest at the outside and working through the tones to the lightest.

Begin with a straight edge and make the long stitches ½ inch and the short ones ¼ inch. Work a short row, placing the stitches close together as shown. Change to the next lighter tone, and work a row of long stitches in the slotted spaces by bringing the needle to the surface through the yarn at the base of each short stitch. Change to a lighter shade and work a row of long stitches in the spaces produced by the last row. Always bring the yarn to the surface through the tip of the stitch of the row above.

An outline of Split Stitch around an area to be worked in Long and Short will impart a raised appearance and a very smooth edge.

OUTLINE STITCH

Outline Stitch creates a fine line of close stitches and can be used as its name suggests or can be worked in rows placed close together to make a pretty filling.

To begin a line of stitching: Bring the needle to the surface at *A* and pull the yarn through. With the yarn above the needle, go down at *B* and come up at *C* exactly halfway between *A* and *B*. Pull the yarn through and continue stitching.

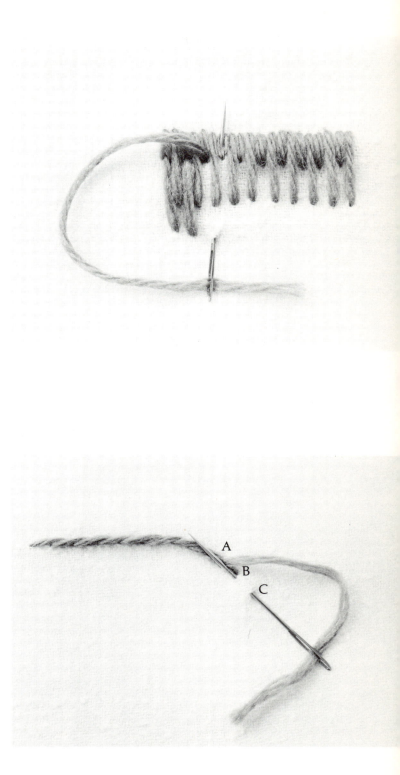

Running Stitch, Whipped

Running Stitch is a basic sewing stitch, good also for embroidery when a fine light line is needed. Work a row of stitches as shown by those in darker thread to make plain Running Stitch. Add a second color by whipping with the lighter color yarn.

To whip: Bring the needle up just under the center of the first Running Stitch. With yarn in position and without piercing the fabric, slide the needle upward under the second stitch. Continue along the row, always inserting the needle upward with the yarn in the position shown.

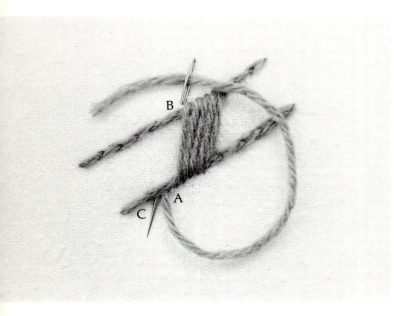

Satin Stitch

One of the loveliest of embroidery stitches, Satin is aptly named, for when properly worked it has a smooth, lustrous look. A Split Stitch outline underneath adds depth and eases the task of making an even outside edge. Extra padding in the form of long stitches can also be added. When Satin Stitch is specified in the embroideries in this book, it is to be padded as shown in the photograph.

To work: Outline the area with Split Stitch in the color that will be used for the Satin Stitch. Begin the Satin Stitch by bringing the needle to the surface at *A* and pulling the yarn through. Make a slanting stitch by taking the needle down at *B* and bringing it up again at *C*, which is close to *A*. Pull the yarn through and continue stitching until the area is covered.

SEEDING

Seeding is ideal as a light filling for flowers, leaves, even backgrounds where just a light texture and a little color are needed.

To work: Make tiny straight stitches and place them at random. The ones shown in the photograph are made double—two stitches in each space. This makes them nice and plump and a little raised. Single stitches should be used where a lighter texture is needed.

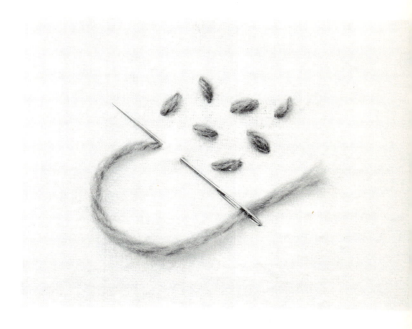

SPIDER WEB, WHIPPED

The Spider Web is usually worked in a circular area. It is a raised stitch which adds a great deal of texture and makes perfect flower centers and other round details. It can be worked with the spokes completely covered or partially exposed. More than one color can be used, so it is possible to shade or contrast within one stitch.

To begin: Place the spokes of the wheel following the letters in Step 1. Next, bring the needle to the surface as close as possible to the center of the spokes in the space between E and D. Without piercing the fabric, slide the needle under two spokes (D and H), as shown in the photograph, and pull the yarn through. Now slide the needle under spokes H and A and pull the yarn through. The yarn has wrapped around spoke H. Repeat, sliding under A and F. Continue around the wheel, always going under one new spoke and the one immediately preceding it. Continue until the stitch is the desired fullness. The more trips around the wheel, the higher the stitch will be.

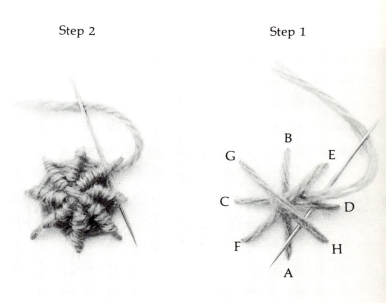

Step 2   Step 1

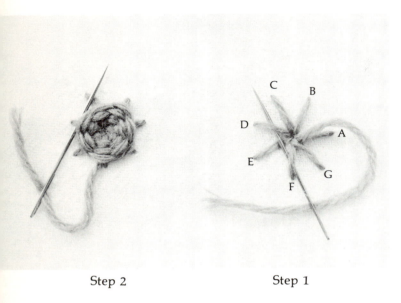

Step 2   Step 1

SPIDER WEB, WOVEN

The Woven Spider Web is not quite as raised as the Whipped, but has a distinctive appearance and can be used in much the same way.

Because it is woven and must be worked on an uneven number of spokes, the foundation is laid out as shown in Step 1 with seven spokes that all end in a center hole. Place them as shown, spacing them evenly. Next, bring the needle to the surface, as close as possible to the center of the wheel, in the space between the spokes A and G. Pull the yarn through. Now, without piercing the fabric, simply weave round and round the wheel—over one, under one, etc.—until the stitch is the fullness desired.

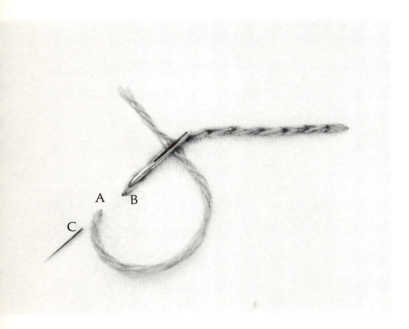

SPLIT STITCH

Hardworking little Split Stitch, which looks like a scaled down version of the Chain, does many embroidery jobs. It is a lovely fine outlining stitch, is often used as padding under other stitches, and can be worked in closely placed rows as a solid filling.

To start: Bring the needle up at A and pull the yarn through. Go down at B and up at C, keeping the space between A and C equal to that between A and B. Pull the thread through, forming a small flat stitch between A and B. Insert the needle down into the center of this stitch, splitting it as shown. Continue in this manner.

STRAIGHT STITCH

The Straight Stitch is an uncomplicated flat stitch often used as an accent or scattered as seeding to add texture to a large, otherwise plain area. The slant and size of the stitches can vary to suit the need.

To work: Simply place the stitches at the desired angle, following the stitching order from *A* to *B* to *C*.

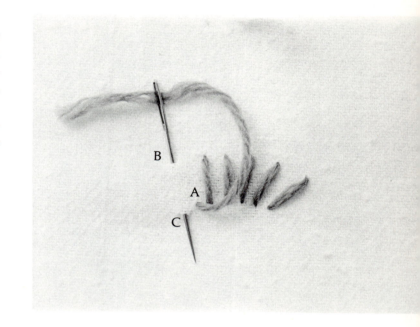

TRELLIS COUCHING

Trellis Couching quickly covers a large area with interesting pattern. The laid and couching threads can be of matching color or of contrasting color. The latter may take the simple upright form shown in the photograph or may be Cross Stitch, Lazy Daisy, or any one of a number of small stitches that would hold the threads in place. The diamond-shaped openings can be left plain as shown, or may be decorated with a small detached stitch.

To begin: Lay the long Straight Stitches in diagonal parallel lines, filling the shape of the motif. Bring the needle threaded with the Couching yarn to the surface at *A* and pull the yarn through. Make the tie-down stitch by inserting the needle at *B* and bringing it up again at *C* in position for the beginning of the next stitch. Tie each intersection of the laid threads in this manner.

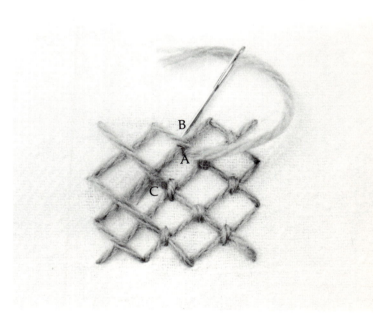

ORIENTAL CRANES

This graceful pair of cranes on an eighteenth-century lacquered cabinet has long been one of my favorite ideas for a crewel picture. An old print stayed in my files for years waiting to be used, until the powder room in a new house needed a light Oriental touch, and the cranes were finally adapted for embroidery.

As in many of the antique Chinese pieces of this genre, the cabinet was lacquered black and the cranes painted soft shades of ivory highlighted with gold. Except for the flowers in the foreground and the crests on the cranes' heads, all other details were metallic gold. It is an elegant composition in the

best Chinese style of the period.

The embroidered adaptation stays very close to the original in composition but departs in coloring. The black background is replaced by a handsome heavy linen of very tight weave. The cranes are still basically ivory with red crests and gold highlights, but the pines have been changed from gold to green, and touches of blue, light green and jade appear where only gold exists in the original. The essential spirit of the old piece remains, but the adaptation has a character all its own—subtle and understated, softly textured and unmistakably Chinese, but at the same time new.

FINISHED SIZE

11 × 16 inches

MATERIALS

Linen, approximately 19 × 24 inches

Persian yarn as follows: 012, Ivory, 4 yards; 438, Buttercup, 1 yard; 468, Yellow White, 17 yards; 467, Light Medium Yellow, 5 yards; 453, Warm Sands, 17 yards; 445, Antique Gold, 5 yards; 442, Saffron, 5 yards; 180, Slate, 11 yards; 520, Hunter Green, 4 yards; 528, Forest Green, 3 yards; 136, Sand, 4 yards; 248, Russet, 7 yards; R-70, Frosted Cherry, 3 yards; 850, Berry, 3 yards; 352, Foam, 2 yards; 367, Light Sea Green, 3 yards; 340, Jade, 3 yards

Framing materials as shown

NOTE

All stitches are to be worked with a single strand of the Persian yarn.

INSTRUCTIONS

Fold a large piece of tracing paper into quarters. Open it flat. Match the fold lines on the paper to the slashed lines on the drawings and trace the four quarters of the design, noting that some portion of the design always overlaps into the adjacent quarter to help place the pieces when the paper is shifted from one drawing to the next. Trace the entire design. Check the alignment and make certain the lines join as they should. Turn the paper over and go over the entire design with a transfer pencil.

Hem or overcast the edges of the linen to prevent fraying. Center the design and transfer it to the linen with a hot iron.

The pine needles are worked entirely in Straight Stitch. Work each fan-shaped group with all stitches intersecting at the base. Work the darkest fans first; then work the lighter ones, letting the stitches fall on top of the darker ones where the two overlap. Only two of the needles of each fan are marked for color, but this is to indicate that the whole group of stitches comprising that fan is to be in the same shade of green.

Work the birds' crests in solid French Knots in color 850. Next, work the bills in Long and Short in 442. Work the tongue of the standing crane in the same stitch in 850. Make the stitches short and use them as a solid filling. Using the Long and Short in the same manner, work the necks in 180, 012, and 438 as indicated. The eyes are Satin Stitch with an outline of tiny Back Stitches and the pupils are 180.

On the crane with the raised head, the throat is to be worked in Long and Short, beginning with 012 in the area nearest the head and working through 468, 467, and 445 to shade toward the back.

The feathers and tails of both birds are to be worked in the following manner (only a few individual feathers have been keyed for color and stitch): Feathers are all Satin Stitch in 438. Work each feather just to the stamped outline, not covering it. This will leave a small void into which the gold outlines are later added. Some of the very small feathers at the neck area will be tedious, but each will take only a couple of stitches. Next, with color 453, work an outline around each feather, using small Split Stitches and pulling the stitches down into the space between the feathers.

Outline the tail feathers with Split Stitch in color 180. Using color 453 and Long and Short, completely fill in all the tail feathers. Then, with 442, add a highlight on top, at the tip of each feather, again using Long and Short. At the base of each feather—where the tail feather joins the body—use color 445 and work a little shading in Long and Short.

On the crane that is bending over, work the upper leg in Long and Short, using small stitches and slanting them to contour the leg. Work the legs and feet as follows:

Standing crane, left leg: Starting at the back top, work a row of Split Stitch from the top of the leg and around the foot to include two of the claws. Next, starting again at the back top, work a row of Split Stitch in color 248 inside the first row and continuing beyond the end of the first to outline the balance of the foot and leg. Repeat with 445. Highlight the leg with a row of 453 down the center and add a few stitches on each claw.

Right leg: Work 180 Split Stitch down the back of the leg and around the two lower claws. Starting again at the top back, work a row of Split Stitch in color 445 inside the first row and continuing around the entire leg and foot. Work a row of 453 inside the outline and then highlight with 442 down the center of the leg and on the claws.

Bending crane: Work the legs in the same manner, making the longer leg correspond to the right leg of the standing crane, the other in the darker shades of the left leg.

The blue under-feathers of the bending crane are to be outlined with Split Stitch in 180, then filled in with Long and Short in the shades of blue noted on the chart.

Work the little Satin Stitch flowers in the colors noted and give each a center French Knot in the color indicated. The larger flat flowers scattered in the foreground are all outlined with Split Stitch in 180, and the inner detail lines are also this stitch. Where Long and Short and several colors are indicated, work the outside edges in the darkest color and work through the other colors from dark to light toward the center to achieve a shaded effect.

The pebbles scattered on the ground are all Satin Stitch in the random colors indicated on the chart. The horizontal landscape lines are "painted" with long Split Stitches placed as noted. Make the stitches a little irregular to enhance the painted effect.

ORIENTAL CRANES

Upper Left Section

Stitches

A Satin
B Long and Short
C Split
D French Knot
E Back

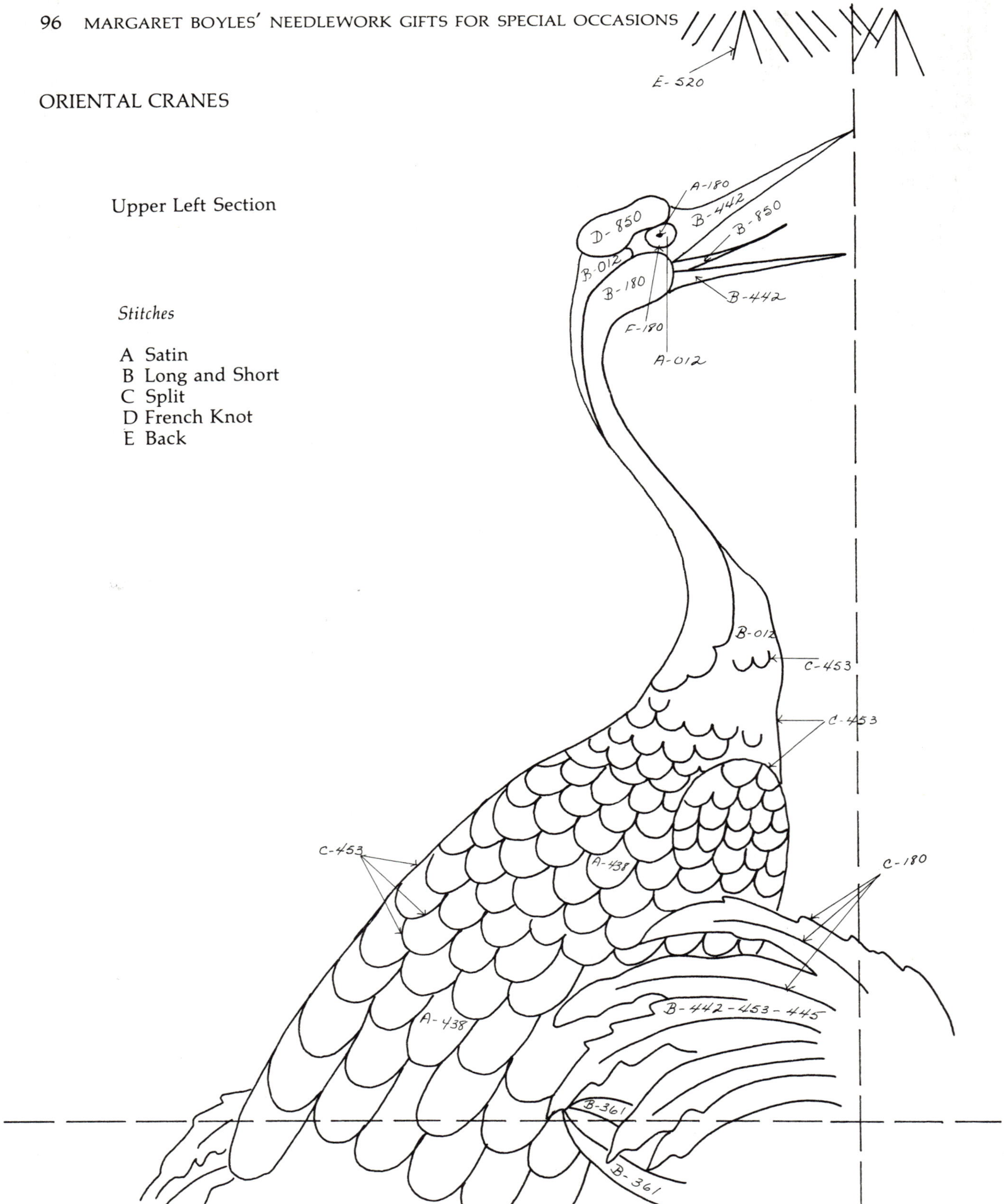

E-520

A-180
B-442
D-850
B-850
B-012
B-180
B-442
F-180
A-012

B-012
C-453

C-453

C-453
A-438
C-180

A-438
B-442-453-445

B-361

B-361

E - 528

Upper Right Section

Colors

012 Ivory
438 Buttercup
468 Yellow White
467 Light Medium Yellow
453 Warm Sands
445 Antique Gold
442 Saffron
180 Slate
520 Hunter Green
528 Forest Green
136 Sand
248 Russet
R-70 Frosted Cherry
850 Berry
352 Foam
367 Light Sea Green
340 Jade

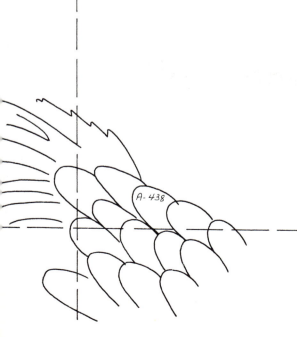

A- 438

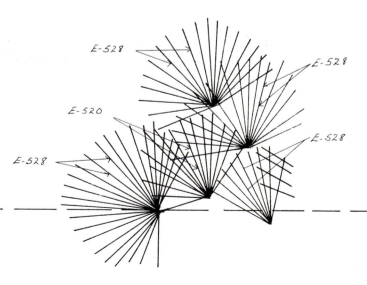

E-528

E-528

E-520

E-528

E-528

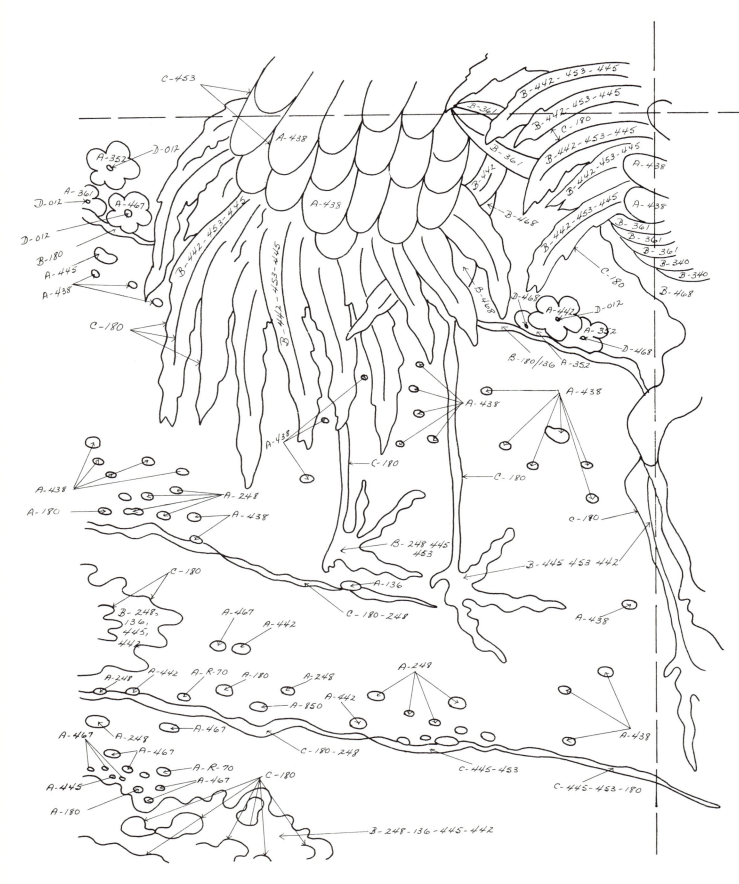

ORIENTAL CRANES

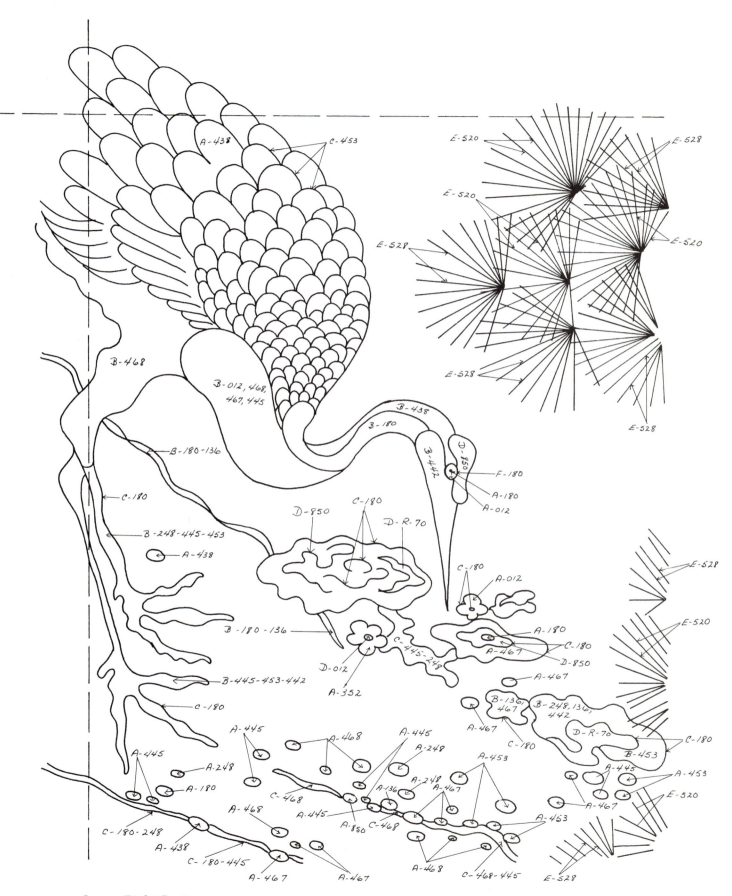

Lower Right Section

PENNSYLVANIA DUTCH WEDDING SAMPLER

In the eighteenth and early nineteenth centuries in that beautiful little section of Pennsylvania known as the Pennsylvania Dutch Country, it was the custom to record births, baptisms, weddings, and deaths with a kind of illuminated manuscript called fraktur. The documents varied greatly, but most recorded some pertinent genealogical information and usually included several religious verses.

Revive that custom with this adaptation of the old form, which adopts the traditional heart-shaped enclosure for the written data and features a wide border decorated with the stylized flowers and birds so dear to the Dutch artists.

This version conceived as a wedding remembrance—the Pennsylvania Dutch called them Trauschein—can also be used as a birth or baptismal record (Taufschein), or adapted for another important event.

FINISHED SIZE
17 × 14 inches

MATERIALS
DMC embroidery floss as follows: 746, Ivory, 1 skein; 727, Yellow, 2 skeins; 725, Gold, 1 skein; 740, Orange, 1 skein; 353, Pale Coral, 2 skeins; 352, Coral, 2 skeins; 351, Deep Coral, 2 skeins; 349, Red, 3 skeins; 3348, Pale Green, 2 skeins; 3347, Medium Green, 2 skeins; 3346, Avocado, 3 skeins; 500 Dark Green, 1 skein; 519, Pale Blue, 2 skeins; 518, Medium Blue, 2 skeins; 517, Bright Blue, 2 skeins; 311, Navy, 1 skein

Linen, approximately 25 × 22 inches
Framing materials as shown

NOTE
Work all stitches with three strands of floss *except* all Outline and all Trellis Couching. For these use only two strands.

INSTRUCTIONS
Fold a large sheet of tracing paper into quarters. Open it flat and place the upper right quadrant over the upper right section of the drawing, matching the fold lines of the paper to the slashed lines on the drawing. Trace that section. Move the paper to the lower right section drawing, match the fold lines to the slashed lines and line up the overlapping portions of the design. Trace that section.

Fold the paper in half lengthwise and trace the left half of the design from the portion already traced. Trace the dotted lines in the heart as a guide for placement of the lettering.

The lettering is simple script, and if you can use your own writing style it will be more personal. If this is not possible, use a sheet of graph paper and plan your lettering on that. Use one line as the base line and trace the letters from the Script alphabet on

Stitches

A Satin
B Chain
C Outline
D Back
E Trellis Couching
F Buttonhole
G Fishbone
H French Knot

Colors

746   Ivory
727   Yellow
725   Gold
740   Orange
353   Pale Coral
352   Coral
351   Deep Coral
349   Red
3348 Pale Green
3347 Medium Green
3346 Avocado
500   Dark Green
519   Pale Blue
518   Medium Blue
517   Bright Blue
311   Navy

PENNSYLVANIA DUTCH WEDDING SAMPLER   Upper Right Section

Lower Right Section

page 152 onto the graph paper, spacing them as they appear on the chart. (If your names and date are short, you may prefer to use the calligraphic alphabet on page 150 to fill the space more completely.)

Trace the planned lettering onto the tracing paper pattern, using the dotted lines for placement.

Turn the finished tracing over and go over all outlines with the transfer pencil—be sure to turn the paper over so the lettering will transfer correctly.

Cut the linen to size; finish the edges to prevent fraying and transfer the design with a hot iron. Place the piece in a hoop and begin the embroidery. Start anywhere that appeals to you.

Work the lettering entirely in Back Stitch in color 3346. If you like use a single strand of color 3347 and whip the Back Stitch for a more rounded look.

Some areas—tulip petals, details on wings and tails of birds, etc.—are marked indicating Satin Stitch. Then arrows indicate that the area is to be outlined and also worked in Trellis Couching—usually in one color. Work the Satin Stitch first with three strands of color. Then, using two strands of the contrasting floss noted, lay the Trellis Couching over the Satin Stitch; fasten the intersections and outline the motif completely with the color noted.

Work the heart in red Satin Stitch; then outline both edges of the line with two strands of dark green and Outline Stitch.

When one or two arrows point to the outlines of a motif and indicate a color and the Outline Stitch, work the color around the entire outside of the motif and also work all interior details even though only one is so denoted.

French Knots and one color indicated in an area mean that the shape is to be filled with the stitches placed close together. Work an outline of Split Stitch in matching color along the outside edges of an area to be worked in Buttonhole Stitch before placing the finishing stitches. Work the Buttonhole Stitches as close together as possible to make a solid filling.

All Satin Stitch is to be worked over an outline of Split Stitch in matching color.

Details of the bird in the upper sections: Work the head in Satin Stitch in the colors indicated; add yellow outlines along the pale blue collar. Work the body in bright blue Chain Stitch, placing the rows close together and following the outlines of the body. Work the yellow Satin Stitch portions of the wings; then add the red Outline Stitch pattern, placing the rows close together. Fill the area completely, using single stitches if necessary. Work the Satin Stitch details of the tail; then outline the entire bird including the wing and all the sections of the tail and head with navy blue. The leaf at the bird's feet is to be pale green Satin Stitch with Trellis Couching on top. The entire leaf is then to be outlined with 3346.

Details of the birds in the lower sections: Work each head, eye, and beak in Satin Stitch. Outline the heads and eyes with 352. Work the bodies in Chain Stitch in 518, medium blue, placing the rows close together to cover the linen. Work each upper tail section in 517, bright blue, also Chain Stitch to cover. The smallest interior section of each wing is to be 351, deep coral Satin Stitch with Trellis

Couching and an outline of orange. The next section of each wing is Satin Stitch in pale blue. The outside wing portion is to be worked in close rows of yellow Outline Stitch, and both this and the pale blue section are to be outlined with navy. Outline the rest of the body with navy.

The center tail section is to be Satin Stitch in 351, deep coral, with Trellis Couching and an outline of orange. The two small side feathers are yellow Satin Stitch outlined with orange.

This design may also be worked in wool yarn if you prefer that look. It will be faster because the wool stitches will be slightly larger, and you may wish to omit the outlining around most of the Satin Stitch.

Don't forget to add your own name or initials and the date in a lower corner to make the remembrance complete.

EMBROIDERED SHEET AND PILLOWCASES

Revive a beautiful Victorian tradition by making a set of hand-embroidered bed linens—a luxury just as appreciated today as in times past. Nothing is more subtle and elegant than white on white and the classic embroidered border complements almost any style bedroom.

Purchase the finest quality percale sheets and pillowcases you can find, keeping up-keep in mind when you buy. All cotton is most desirable, but unless it has been treated so that it does not need ironing, it will proba-bly come out of the dryer a mass of wrinkles and your beautiful gift will spend most of its days folded on a shelf of the linen closet. There is a beautiful blend of 50 percent cotton, 50 percent polyester in a very fine thread count percale that looks and feels as luxurious as the all-natural fiber, but it is easy-care and infinitely more practical. It is made by most of the major linen producers and should be easy to locate.

The custom finishing touches—side hems and hand-applied lace—coupled with the embroidery make these sheets and pillowcases the equal of those found in the most exclusive linen boutiques. Enjoy making them and then enjoy using them yourself or giving them as a wedding or anniversary gift that will be remembered and used for many years.

FINISHED SIZE
Sheet, 81 × 104 inches (standard full size. See instructions for information about other sizes.)
Pillowcase, 21 × 33 inches

MATERIALS
Standard full-size flat sheet with 4-inch hems
One pair of standard size pillowcases with 4-inch hems
White cotton embroidery floss, 18 skeins (10 for sheet, 4 for each pillowcase)
Heavy cotton lace, 12 yards

NOTE
Work all embroidery stitches with three strands of floss.

INSTRUCTIONS
Sheet: Use the wrong side of the sheet as the right side. By hand, whip the lace to both edges of the hem. Cut off the side selvages and finish each side with a 1-inch machine-stitched hem.

Instructions are for a standard full-size sheet. You can adapt for twin, queen or king by changing the number of repeats in the garland. Estimate the needs for embroidery floss and lace accordingly. The embroidered garland does not extend all the way to the side hems.

For best results use a pale pink or blue transfer pencil, and make sure it is one that washes out after the embroidery is complete because transfer lines are a little more apparent when both fabric and thread are pure white.

Draw a horizontal line on tracing paper and match it to the slashed lines on the drawings, using it to line up the sections of the garland both in tracing and later in transferring to the fabric. Use the dotted stems at the top of the flowers as a guide to joining the sections of the garland.

Section 1

Section 2

For the double sheet a garland of ten flowers beginning and ending with a flower without a stem attached (as in the small drawing) is needed. This works out to be four repeats of the full garland plus one which ends with the flower portion only of section 2. When the garland is placed on the sheet, the leaf of section 1 falls on the center fold line of the sheet and the garland extends to within 11 inches of the side hems.

Transferring the long garland to the sheet is easier if five separate copies of the repeat are made and applied one at a time rather than attempting to handle one long strip of tissue. To place the design, fold the sheet in half vertically and mark the fold line. Make a very light guideline about 2 inches from the top hem and match the pencilled line on the transfer to it.

Before transferring, pin the tissues in place to make sure they are centered and arranged as needed. Begin with one repeat placed so the leaf of section 1 is on the fold line. Use two complete repeats on the left and one plus the flower of section 2 on the right. Transfer.

All stitches are to be worked with three strands of embroidery floss. Pad all Satin Stitch with an outline of Split Stitch. Every black line on the drawing is to be worked in Outline Stitch except around the three Fishbone leaves on section 2.

Pillowcase: To make the wrong side of the pillowcase usable turn the seam at the top and side into a French seam by stitching over the existing seam from the right side. Sew lace to both edges of the case to match the trim on the sheet.

Trace the design sections to make a garland of three flowers like that shown on the small drawing. Center it and transfer to the pillowcase, placing it 2 inches from the hem as on the sheet. Embroider with the same stitches as the sheet.

CHINESE BUTTERFLY PILLOW

The butterfly, which is the symbol of joy to the Chinese, appears in many beautiful and graceful forms in their art. These, with their flowing assymetrical shapes were embroidered in large numbers on an old robe. On the garment they were worked primarily in Satin Stitch with touches of the fabled Forbidden Stitch; to reproduce them use Satin Stitch, French Knots and a few little details of Outline Stitch. The classic fret borders and contains them.

The same butterflies in the flamboyant colors of the original robe were also adapted for a needlepoint pillow—Peking Butterflies on page 44—to allow canvas embroiderers the pleasure of re-creating them.

FINISHED SIZE

14 × 14 inches

MATERIALS

    Persian yarn as follows: 456, Baby Yellow,
       5 yards; G-64, Spring Apple Green, 22
       yards; 574, Seaweed, 4 yards; G-74,
       Light Apple Green, 33 yards; 414, Rust,
       2 yards
    White fabric, ½ yard (wool serge as
       shown, linen or other tightly woven
       white fabric)

NOTE

Work all stitches with a single strand of
yarn.

INSTRUCTIONS

Fold a sheet of tracing paper into quarters
and trace one section of the drawing into
each quarter. Be extra careful when tracing
the fret and border outline to draw the lines
perfectly. You may prefer to use a transparent
graph paper with a ten-to-the-inch grid
for tracing this design. It will ensure a perfect
border.

Cut an 18-inch square from one end of the
fabric and stamp the design on it. Make the
pillow back and self-piping from the remaining
piece of fabric.

Measure out 1½ inches from the outside
border and mark the cutting line for the pillow.
After the embroidery is completed and
blocked, cut on this line. Use the trimmed
piece as a pattern for cutting the pillow back.

Most of the embroidery is Satin Stitch.
Note that on the drawings these areas bear
only a color notation. Areas to be worked in
French Knots and Outline Stitch are marked
accordingly. Work all others in Satin Stitch.

Pad all Satin Stitch with an outline of Split
Stitch in matching color. When working the
fret and border outline, begin and end all
yarn strands on the right side. Do not cut off
tag ends; hold them in place and work the
Satin Stitch over them for extra padding.

If you work the Satin Stitches on a slant,
the corners of the fret and border will look
nicer and it will take fewer stitches than if
the stitches were laid straight across the
lines.

CHINESE BUTTERFLY PILLOW

Upper Left Section

Stitches

A Satin
B Outline
C French Knot

Upper Right Section

Colors

1 #456 Baby Yellow
2 #G-74 Light Apple Green
3 #574 Seaweed
4 #G-64 Spring Apple Green
5 #414 Rust

CHINESE BUTTERFLY PILLOW

Lower Left Section

Lower Right Section

OVAL MINIATURES

This charming pair of oval miniature pictures took only a few evenings' work and a minimum of money, but they were the hit of the day at the wedding shower at which they were given. Worked in delicate stitches and soft neutrals on bold green linen, they feature flowers like we usually associate with crewel, but these have been worked with cotton embroidery floss to allow more detail in the small designs. The result is a finely textured embroidery that fits beautifully into the little oval frames.

The designs can be framed as shown or used as trimming on apparel or linens. Also think about changing colors and background for a different look. The neutral embroidery colors shown would be lovely on a white or unbleached linen; bright flower colors would also be very attractive; think also about three shades of blue on white or the three colors used here on dark brown fabric—the possibilities are endless.

FINISHED SIZE
3¼ × 4¼ inches

MATERIALS
   Two pieces linen, each about 7 × 9 inches
   Cotton embroidery floss, one skein each:
      ecru, beige, and warm brown
   Two oval frames, 4 × 5 inches

NOTE
Separate the embroidery thread and work all stitches with three strands except in the minor instances noted.

INSTRUCTIONS
Trace the designs, center and transfer them to the linen. Note that the linen sizes given are the minimum sizes that can be used. If you have used pieces this small, you will want to add muslin side pieces so you can place the embroidery into a hoop for working. See page 79 for comments on this process.

Flower #1: Space the French Knots and Seed Stitches in the flower and leaf as indicated by the dots and short lines on the drawing. Work Trellis Couching in the flower center with ecru, then tie down at the intersections with a single strand of brown. Outline this section with Chain Stitch in beige.

Shade the Long and Short flower petals from light at the tips to dark at the base, using all three colors of floss. Shade the leaf at the lower left with rows of Split Stitch by working the vein with a single row of brown, following this with a row of beige on each side of the vein. Then complete the leaf by filling in all the remaining space with ecru.

Flower #2

Flower #1

Colors

1 Ecru
2 Beige
3 Brown

Stitches

A Satin
B Outline
C French Knot
D Long and Short
E Seed
F Trellils Couching
G Split
H Chain

Flower #2: Space the French Knots in the leaf as shown by the dots, but work them solid to fill all the space of the bud. Shade the Long and Short portion of the flower from light at the top of the point to dark at the base, using all three shades of thread. Outline the upper flower section with shade #2, beige. Then work Trellis Couching in the section with ecru and tie it down at the intersections with a single strand of brown.

After the large Satin Stitch petals have been worked in ecru, work Trellis Couching with a single strand of brown over the Satin Stitch and also outline these petals with a single strand of brown and the Outline Stitch. The petals at the base and sides of the flowers, which are shown to be worked in Outline Stitch, should be worked solid to fill the space.

Block the completed embroidery and mount in oval frames as shown. If you like a softer look in framed embroidery pieces, place a piece of polyester quilt filler under the linen before inserting it into the frames.

EMBROIDERED LINEN PICTURE FRAME

After much work printing, restoring and painting this precious picture of my mother at age three, I decided it needed a very special frame. Naturally, embroidery was my first thought, and this daintily embellished and padded oval with its myriad tiny flowers seemed just right.

I constructed the entire frame, cutting the components from cardboard, padding the top with quilt filler and covering the back and easel with plain linen. You could, however, use the pattern to cover a mat and use it in a standard 5- × 7-inch frame.

FINISHED SIZE
Frame, 5 × 7 inches
Oval mat opening, 3 × 4 inches

MATERIALS
Heavyweight cardboard, 12 × 7 inches
Natural linen, 15 × 12 inches
Six-strand cotton embroidery floss, one skein each color: light blue, medium blue, dark blue, light yellow, medium yellow, orange, pale pink, medium pink, coral, light green, medium green

NOTE
Separate the embroidery floss and work all stitches with three strands.

INSTRUCTIONS

Fold the tracing paper into quarters. Open it flat; match the fold lines to the dashed lines on the chart. Trace the fold lines, cutting line, and oval lines as a series of small dots. Trace the flowers in the lower quarter as shown. Fold the paper again on the fold lines and copy the flowers in the other three sections. Turn the paper over and trace the entire design with a transfer pencil.

On the straight of the material, carefully cut the linen 10 × 12 inches. Fold it into quarters and press. Open it flat; place the transfer design on the linen, matching fold lines and transfer with a hot iron.

Separate the thread and work all stitches with three strands, following the chart for color and stitch placement. Note that the small Bullion Stitch rosebuds have been shown on the chart as little donut-shaped motifs. Some of these are marked with a series of parallel lines, some are dotted, and the remainder are plain. The lined ones are to be worked in three shades of pink; dotted ones are to be yellow and orange, while the plain ones are to be worked in the three shades of blue.

To make a rosebud, begin with two stitches of the darkest shade lying side by side as shown in the detail drawing. Place a longer stitch of the next lighter hue on each side of the center stitches. Finish the flower with closely placed stitches of the lightest shade. Wrap the needle with a coil of thread longer than the finished stitch should be, and the result will be stitches that curve to form the rosebud shape.

The small dots scattered on the background are all to be worked as French Knots.

Use pink, blue, green and yellow, and just place the colors in a random pattern to please yourself.

Using the drawing as a guide, cut two 5- × 7-inch pieces of cardboard and cut the oval opening in one. With one of the thick white craft glues, fasten Dacron quilt filling to the cardboard with the opening.

Block the embroidered linen and trim the outside edges back to the cutting line. Carefully cut out the oval opening in the embroidered piece, cutting on a line 1 inch inside the oval fold line. Then cut from the cut edge almost to the fold line making five or six slashes in each quarter. Be careful to clip almost to the line, so the edges will turn back neatly, but the cuts will not be visible on the right side.

Place the embroidery on padded cardboard, center it, and pull the raw edges to the back of the cardboard. Glue it in place, pulling the fabric tightly enough to make a neat edge, but not so tightly that the padding is flattened.

Cut an easel shape from cardboard, cover it with linen, and fasten it to the cardboard back, using a piece of fabric as a hinge. Cover the back with linen. Insert the picture and tape it into place. Glue the front to the back.

Notes

Dots (∴) are French Knots (see instructions for colors).

 Bullion Stitch Rosebud
3 shades of blue

 Bullion Stitch Rosebud
2 yellow shades with orange

 Bullion Stitch Rosebud
3 shades of pink

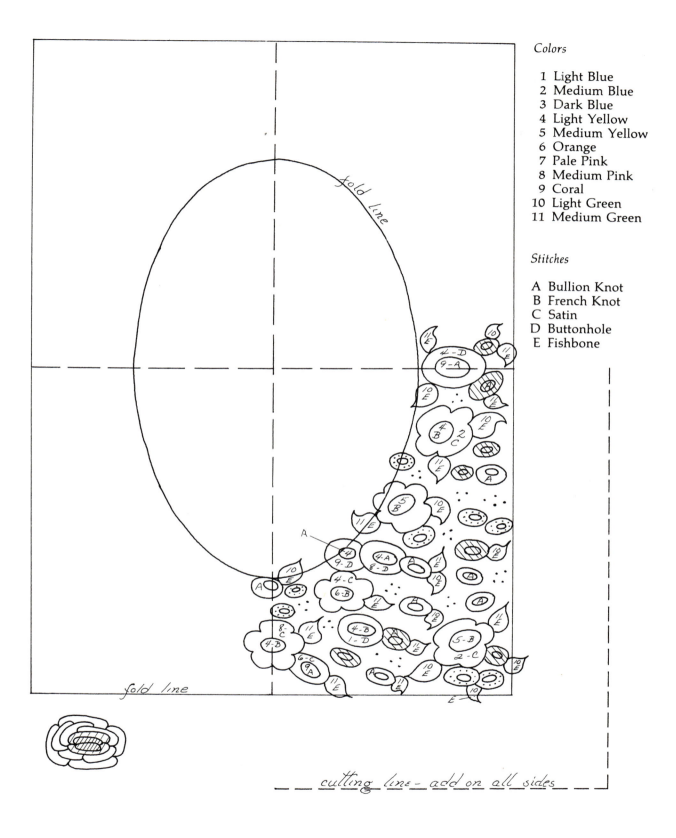

Colors

1 Light Blue
2 Medium Blue
3 Dark Blue
4 Light Yellow
5 Medium Yellow
6 Orange
7 Pale Pink
8 Medium Pink
9 Coral
10 Light Green
11 Medium Green

Stitches

A Bullion Knot
B French Knot
C Satin
D Buttonhole
E Fishbone

fold line

fold line

cutting line - add on all sides

124

PLACEMAT AND NAPKIN SET

Ecru embroidery on pristine white linen makes placemats and napkins pretty enough to be used with the finest china. Begin with finished linen mats and napkins or make your own; embroider and trim them with heavy cotton lace. Surprise the bride with a set of two for special romantic occasions or give eight for elegant dinner parties.

The pictured mat and napkin were purchased in a department store linen section. Made of a blended linen and polyester fabric, the placemat has a 1½-inch hem, the napkin a machine-finished rolled hem. The lace resembles old Irish crochet and was simply whipped to the finished edges of each. A 1¼-inch-wide version was used on the placemat while a ½-inch-wide matching piece edges the napkin. A single row of Whipped Running Stitch in ecru embroidery thread hides the machine-stitched hem of the placemat and adds an interesting bit of color on the border.

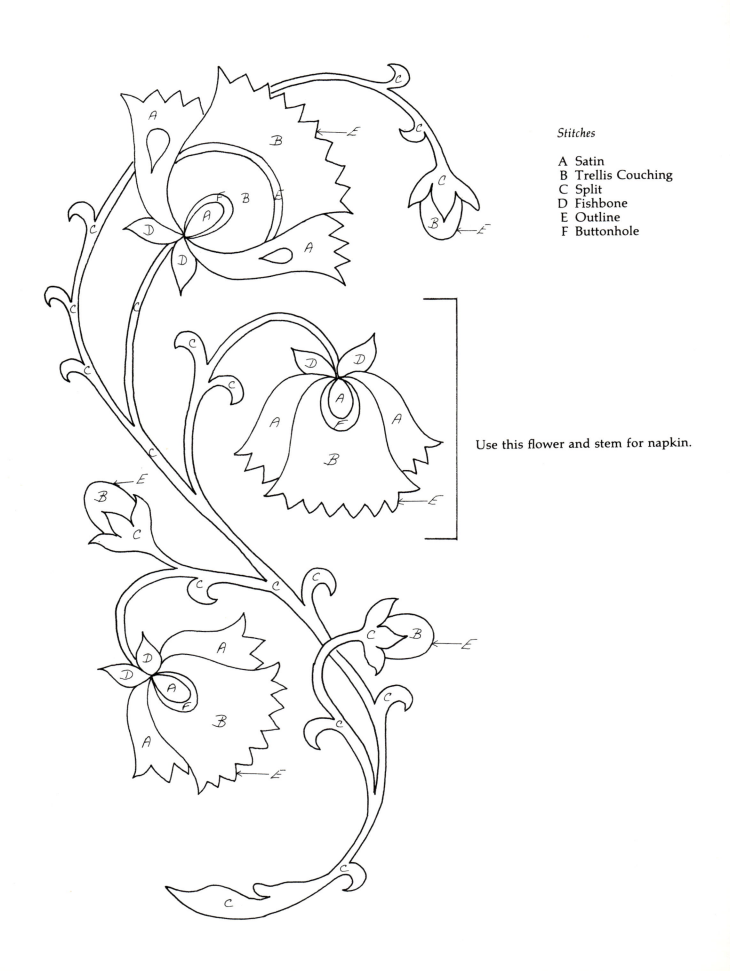

Stitches

A Satin
B Trellis Couching
C Split
D Fishbone
E Outline
F Buttonhole

Use this flower and stem for napkin.

FINISHED SIZE
Placemat, 13 × 18 inches
Napkin, 16 × 16 inches

MATERIALS
(Quantities are for one placemat and one napkin.)
One white placemat, 13 × 18 inches
One matching napkin, 16 × 16 inches
Six-strand embroidery floss, ecru color, 6 skeins
1½-inch-wide white cotton lace, 64 inches
½-inch-wide white cotton lace, 65 inches

NOTE
Separate embroidery floss and work all stitches with three strands.

INSTRUCTIONS
Placemat: With a pencil trace the embroidery motif. Turn the drawing over and go over the outlines with a transfer pencil. With an iron transfer the drawing to the linen, placing the motif on the left side of the mat so that the top, bottom and sides are equidistant from the edges.

Embroider, using three strands of floss and the stitches noted on the chart. If your placemat has a machine-stitched hem as this one did, work a row of Whipped Running Stitch over the stitching. If the mat is finished with a rolled hem (or other narrow finish) place the Whipped Running Stitch 1½ inches from the finished edge.

Napkin: With a pencil trace only the flower and stem noted for use on the napkin. Place on one corner of the napkin as shown in the picture and transfer the design. Embroider with the same stitches as on the placemat.

If any traces of the transfer lines remain in the finished work, wash it by hand in warm water. Do not wring. Roll it in a towel and iron it dry, following the instructions for blocking crewel embroidery on page 155.

With sewing thread and small invisible stitches, whip the lace to the hem edges of the placemat and napkin.

LOCOMOTIVE PILLOW TOY

More than a rectangular pillow with a picture of an engine embroidered on it, this pillow is shaped like the locomotive itself to intrigue little engineers—perhaps even some grown ones! The design is stamped on unbleached muslin, colored with fabric markers, and then embellished with touches of embroidery. Lots of effect from a minimum of work. This combination of paint and embroidery stitches is a useful tool and one you will find other uses for once you have discovered how much fun it is to use.

Choose the pens or paints for this carefully. Look for felt-tip pens made especially

JACOBEAN NEEDLEPOINT PILLOW, page 29

BARGELLO IN A CONTEMPORARY MOOD, page 59

CARNATION PILLOW, page 70

ORIENTAL CRANES, page 93

CHRISTMAS SNOWFLAKES, page 48

CHRISTMAS CRYSTALS, page 51

MINIATURE SAMPLERS, page 135

SCHOOLGIRL'S SAMPLER, page 145

BIRTH RECORD SAMPLER, page 140

PENNSYLVANIA DUTCH WEDDING SAMPLER,
page 100

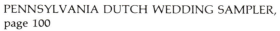

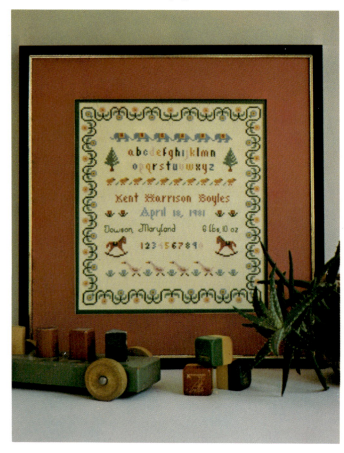

PASTEL BARGELLO PINCUSHION,
page 63

GEOMETRIC NEEDLEPOINT PINCUSHIONS,
page 36

EMBROIDERED SHEET AND PILLOWCASES,
page 106

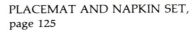

PLACEMAT AND NAPKIN SET,
page 125

LOCOMOTIVE PILLOW TOY, page 128

EMBROIDERED LINEN PICTURE FRAME, page 121

OVAL MINIATURES, page 116

ROMAN STRIPE THREE-PIECE SET, page 66

BARGELLO EYEGLASS CASE, page 56

ARAN TEXTURED TOTE, page 53

BUTTERFLY GRAPHIC, page 40

for use on fabric. They contain a special ink or dye that will not run and bleed beyond the space you want to color—it is not enough that the ink be permanent because it can still bleed badly into adjacent areas. There are also ball-point paint tubes made specifically for "liquid embroidery" that can be used. If you elect to use the latter, apply a thin coat of paint to the fabric because a heavy one will be difficult to embroider through.

Practice coloring the fabric on a scrap to learn how to apply a smooth coat of dye and to be sure your paints are going to fill areas without bleeding. It is also a good idea to test the sample for water fastness to make sure all the colors are permanent. Do this by wetting the sample, drying it on a white paper towel, or ironing it dry between two pieces of white fabric.

FINISHED SIZE
10 × 13 inches

MATERIALS
 Unbleached muslin, ½ yard
 Fabric marking pens or ball-point tubes for liquid embroidery in the following colors: light blue, medium blue, yellow, gray, red and medium green
 Persian yarn as follows: 005, White, 1 yard; 456, Baby Yellow, 5 yards; 242, Red, 5 yards; 528, Forest Green, 3 yards; 853, Flesh, ½ yard; 756, Summer Blue, 3 yards; 752, Medium Blue, 5 yards; 184 Silver Gray, 3 yards; 217, Wood Brown, ½ yard

NOTE
Separate the yarn and work all stitches with a single strand.

 The colors of the paint and the yarn do not match exactly.

Stitches

A Satin
B Chain
C Spider Web, Woven
D Outline
E Herringbone
F Back
G Seed
H Straight
J Trellis Couching

Colors

005 White
456 Baby Yellow
242 Red
528 Forest Green
853 Flesh
756 Summer Blue
752 Medium Blue
184 Silver Gray
217 Wood Brown

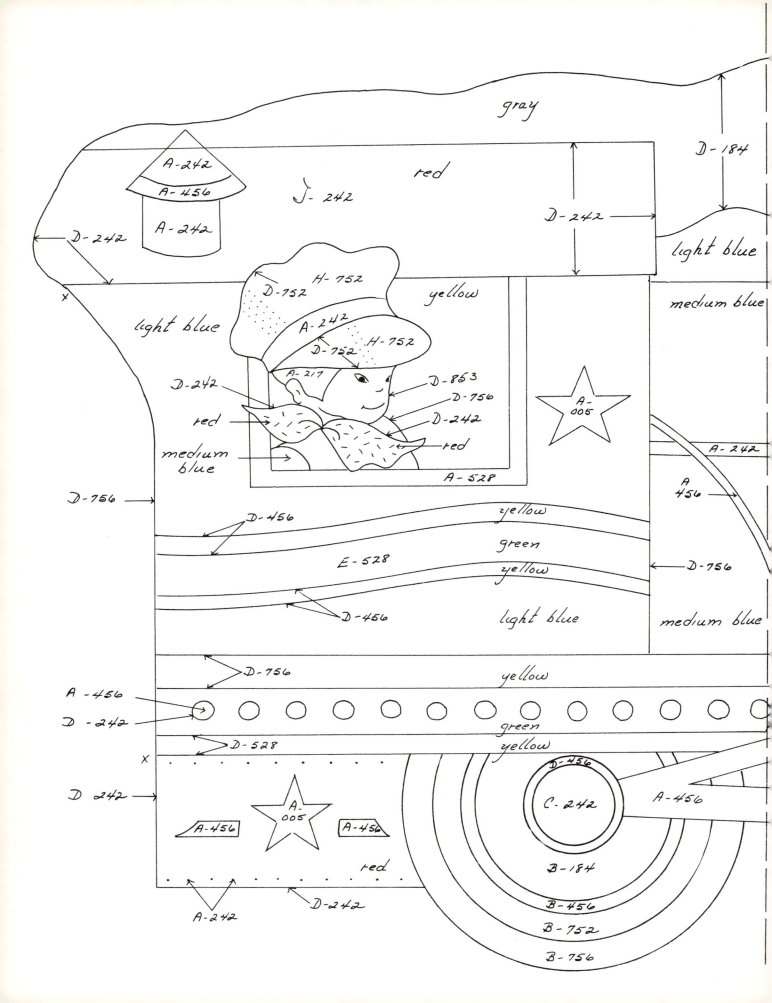

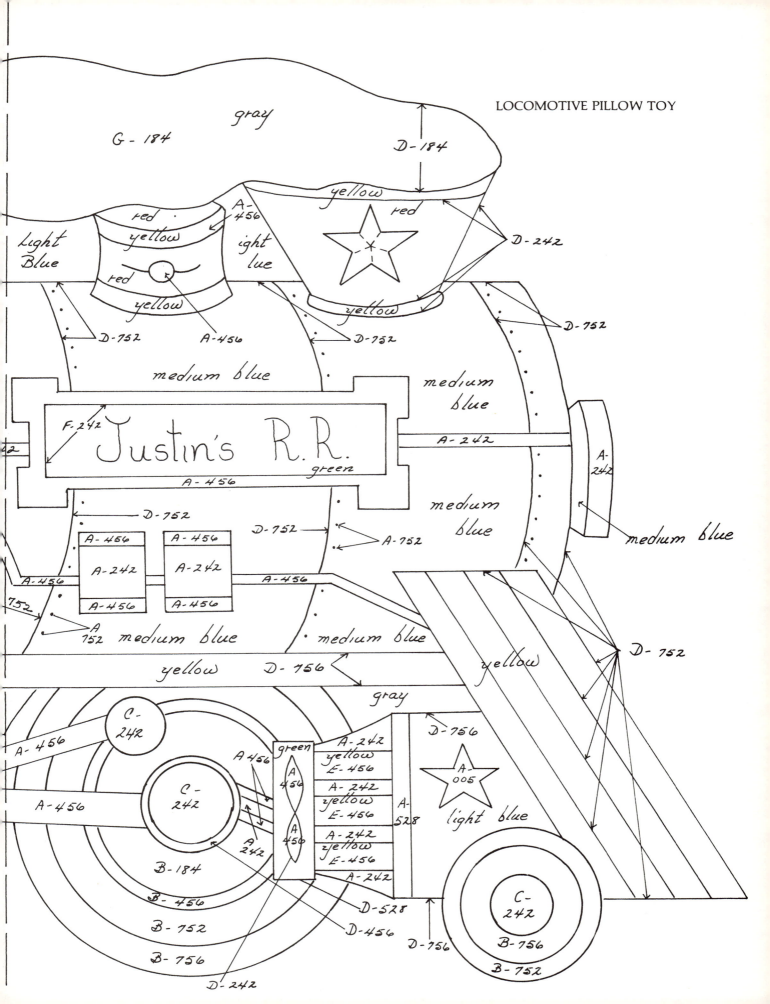

INSTRUCTIONS

Fold a sheet of tracing paper in half vertically. Match the fold lines to the slashed line on the drawings and trace the locomotive. Turn the tracing paper over and go over all outlines with the transfer pencil. Center the tracing·on an 18-inch square of unbleached muslin and transfer it to the fabric with a hot iron. Keep the rectangular shape through the embroidery and blocking processes and trim as instructed when the pillow is being constructed.

Stretch the fabric in a large roller frame or use stretcher strips large enough to have the entire design exposed. With the markers or ball-point paint tubes, color the portions of design that have written color notations on them in the drawings in the book. Not all areas need to be colored—for example, those that are to be covered with Satin Stitch. I have found it easier to get an even coat of color when the fabric is stretched tightly on a frame or the stretcher strips. If you feel you can work better without, place the fabric on a piece of absorbent paper to catch any color that might bleed through and damage the surface underneath.

Most of the embroidery consists of adding touches of color and texture by outlining areas and filling others completely with embroidery. For instance, the smoke is outlined in gray, and the interior area is filled with a sprinkling of little Seed Stitches for texture; the locomotive roof is outlined in red, then filled in with Trellis Couching laid in a diagonal pattern, with the rows placed about ½ inch apart and fastened with an upright red stitch. The smoke stack is red and yellow Satin Stitch.

Work all the stars in white Satin Stitch, working it in a pattern indicated by the dotted lines on the star in the largest smoke stack. Outline the section of the engine body in blue and work the little rivets in several Satin Stitches close together to make a raised spot. The cow-catcher is to be colored yellow and all outlines are to be worked in medium blue Outline Stitch.

Start working the wheels by making the Woven Spider Web center, then working outward in concentric rows, following the outline of the wheels and filling the spaces completely.

Where the Herringbone Stitch is used in the stripes, make the stitches as wide as the stripe and work them widely spaced so they add texture but do not fill the area completely.

Outline the engineer's cap with medium blue; then lay Straight Stitches in a striped pattern, following the dotted lines to give the effect of traditional railroad gear. Outline the face in flesh, use a few red Outline Stitches for the mouth, a few Straight Stitches for the eyes and nose, Satin Stitch for the hair. Outline the kerchief in red, then add white Seeding in the pattern shown by the little straight lines on the chart. Outline the shirt sections with medium blue. Make the window frame green Satin Stitch.

The dots along the bottom of the engine body at the back are circular Satin Stitch areas outlined with red.

Block the completed embroidery. Use the remainder of the unbleached muslin for the pillow back. Place the embroidered section on top of the backing fabric, right sides together. Pin. With the embroidered piece on top, stitch the two together beginning at the "X" on the back of the engine body and ending at the "X" at the edge of the roof. Stitch carefully along the outlines of the engine, using the lines of the back of the embroidery stitches as a guide and placing the machine stitches just outside the embroidery so that no fabric will show beyond the stitches but the embroidery will not be taken up in the machine stitching. Carefully trim, leaving about ½-inch seam allowances in most places, but trimming close to the stitching at the corners so the shapes can be turned easily. Clip along the curves as necessary.

Stuff, beginning with the headlight and cow-catcher and using small amounts of fiberfilling at a time. Use the eraser end of a pencil to push the filling into the corners if necessary. Give the pillow a good firm filling and then slip-stitch the opening to finish.

MINIATURE SAMPLERS

Four little samplers patterned after eighteenth-century schoolgirls' pieces make a lovely gift. Make one or two or all four for the new bride, a good friend's birthday or a special Christmas or wedding anniversary gift—or make them for yourself and enjoy them in almost any room in the house.

If you've never tried Counted Cross Stitch, the small size of these samplers makes them an ideal first project. Read the basic instructions and enjoy a new experience. Once you've worked Cross Stitch from a chart and found how easy it is and how much more accurate than stamped work, you'll never go back to the latter.

The colors in the photographed models are predominately pastels: two pinks, two blues, two greens and an antique gold. All seven colors are used on each sampler to make a matched set on a very white Hardanger fabric. Change to bright colors and a yellow background, harvest colors on beige, or shades of beige and brown on a natural fabric for different looks.

If you prefer canvas work to Cross Stitch, use the designs for needlepoint. The thread count of the canvas will affect the finished size of the piece. Quickpoint canvas would be very attractive; a #10 mesh canvas will make up as a 5- × 7-inch picture.

FINISHED SIZE
5 × 7 inches

MATERIALS
22-thread count white Hardanger fabric, four pieces, at least 9 × 11 inches
Cotton embroidery floss, one skein each: antique gold, pale pink, medium pink, pale blue, medium blue, light green, dark green
Four picture frames, 5 × 7 inches

NOTE
Separate the embroidery floss and work all stitches with three strands.

INSTRUCTIONS
Cut the fabric and stitch the edges to prevent fraying. Begin working either at the top or bottom center border, working first the green vine and then adding the blossoms. Next, work the body of the design, placing it within the framework of the border as shown on the charts. On the "Home" sampler, outline the window panes with one vertical and two horizontal long stitches. Make the tail of the dog also with Straight Stitches as charted.

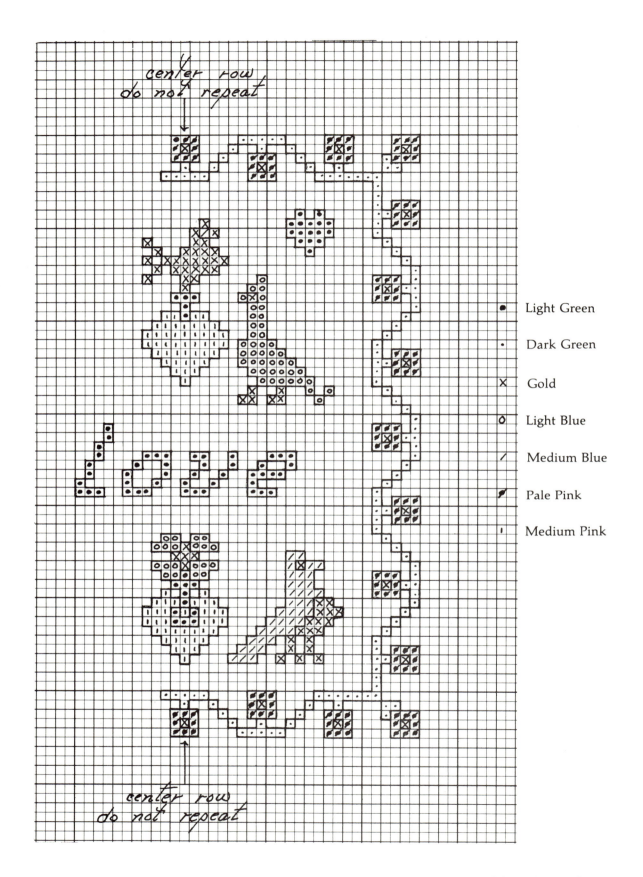

Light Green
Dark Green
Gold
Light Blue
Medium Blue
Pale Pink
Medium Pink

MINIATURE SAMPLERS

center row
do not repeat

Light Green

Dark Green

Gold

Light Blue

Medium Blue

Pale Pink

Medium Pink

center row
do not repeat

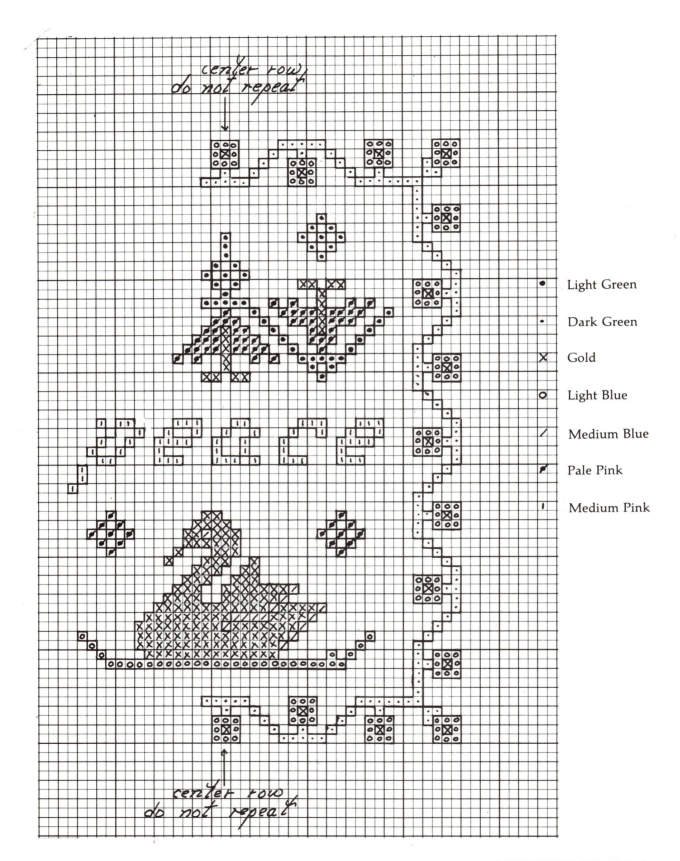

center row)
do not repeat

Light Green

Dark Green

Gold

Light Blue

Medium Blue

Pale Pink

Medium Pink

center row
do not repeat

MINIATURE SAMPLERS

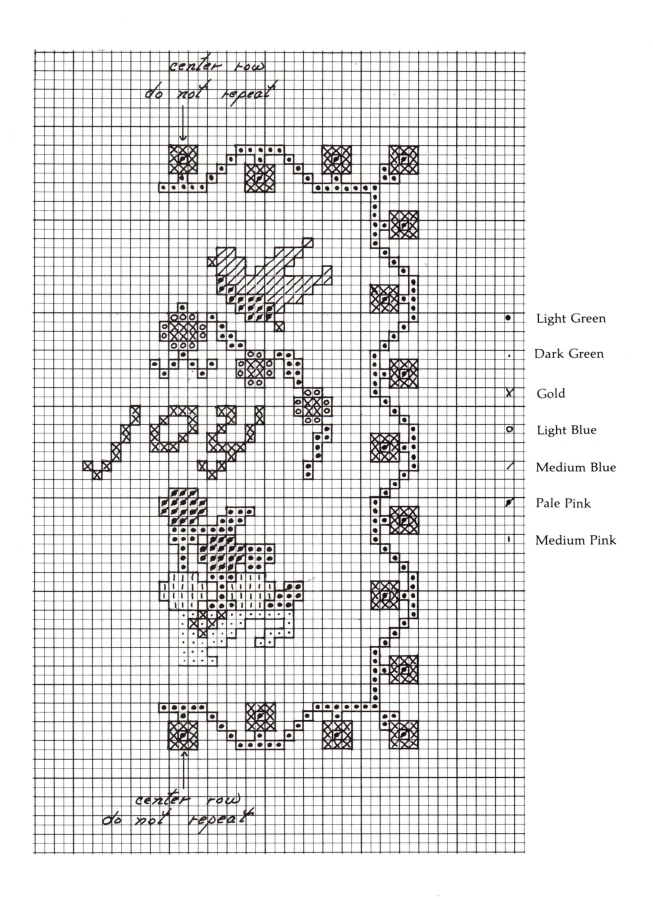

center row
do not repeat

Light Green
Dark Green
Gold
Light Blue
Medium Blue
Pale Pink
Medium Pink

center row
do not repeat

BIRTH RECORD SAMPLER

A parade of chubby blue circus elephants, a row of noisy pink geese, and a line of pert baby chicks march to announce the happy news that a baby has arrived! Crayon-bright embroidery floss on a background of yellow Hardanger makes this a cheerful addition to the nursery and is a gift parents will cherish.

Although it is Counted Cross Stitch, the motifs and lettering are uncomplicated, making this a fairly easy and quick piece to work. Take the time to add your name or initials and the date to make the record complete. You can use the space in the lower corners either inside or outside the border for this final touch.

140

FINISHED SIZE
11¾ × 13½ inches

MATERIALS

    22-thread count yellow Hardanger fabric, at least 16 × 18 inches

    DMC cotton embroidery floss as follows: 727, Bright Yellow, 1 skein; 741, Orange, 1 skein; 350, Cherry Red, 1 skein; 891, Coral, 1 skein; 761, Pink, 1 skein; 975, Warm Brown, 1 skein; 813, Light Blue, 1 skein; 826, Medium Blue, 1 skein; 701, Medium Green, 2 skeins; 368, Light Green, 2 skeins

    Mats and framing materials as shown (This custom-size frame was made at home following instructions and suggestions on page 121.)

NOTE

Separate the embroidery floss and work all stitches with three strands.

Work all stitches over a square of four threads so the stitches count eleven to the inch.

INSTRUCTIONS

Cut the fabric and stitch along the edges to prevent fraying. With sewing thread place a basting stitch line through both the vertical and horizontal center row lines of the fabric to correspond to those marked on the chart.

Using the alphabets on page 144, lay out the baby's name on graph paper, spacing the letters as shown on the chart. Count the spaces used and mark the center row. Move down the number of spaces shown on the chart and work out the birth date, centering it under the baby's name. The two little flowers at the end of the date on the finished piece are spacers. If your date is longer, you may be able to use just one; if the date is shorter, you can add an extra flower.

The name used on the finished birth certificate is fairly long, but if yours is longer, you have two options: use only the first and last names, or widen the entire piece to accommodate the name. Note that the horizontal sections of the flower garland at the top and bottom of the piece is five stitches wide at the center. This can be repeated again as many times as needed on either side to widen the piece. If you add several wide sections, you may want to add a flower at the end of the rows where they are used, and you may want to move the trees and rocking horses a couple of threads toward the border to balance the design. I suggest that if you do have to add width, plan it first on graph paper. It is easier to erase than to rip out stitches.

Lay out the stitches for the birthplace and weight, centering them under the date and spacing as shown on the chart. These stitches are just Straight Stitches laid out on the fabric exactly as shown on the charts.

When the personal information is charted, you can begin working. Begin with the border at the center of either the top or side and lay out the bright green garland. I like to start at the top and work down, placing the row of elephants and then going on to the alphabet and continuing down.

Only about half of the alphabets and numerals are shown on the charts. These are to be laid out as started on the chart and continued with the aid of those on page 144. Spacing is the same on both charts to make transition easy.

Colors for the letters and numerals not

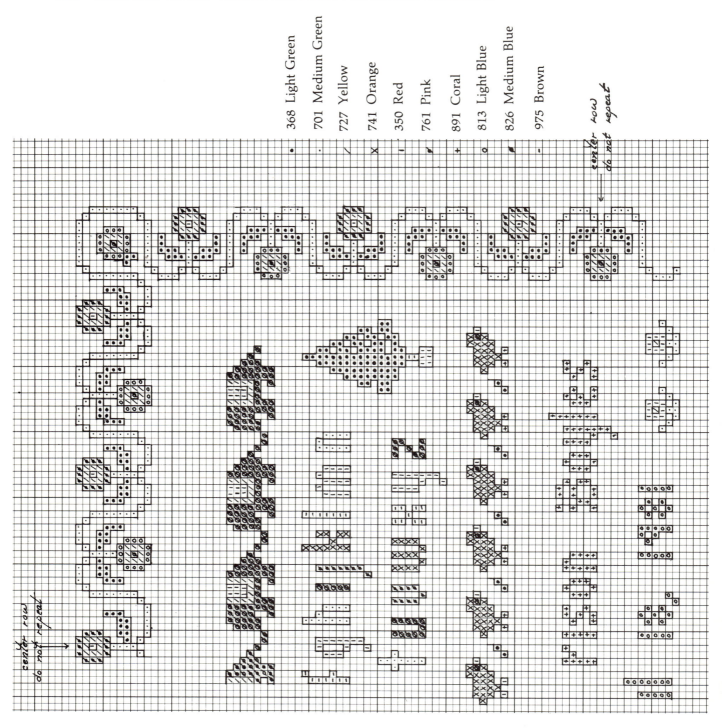

368 Light Green
701 Medium Green
727 Yellow
741 Orange
350 Red
761 Pink
891 Coral
813 Light Blue
826 Medium Blue
975 Brown

center row
do not repeat

center row
do not repeat

BIRTH RECORD SAMPLER

Upper Section

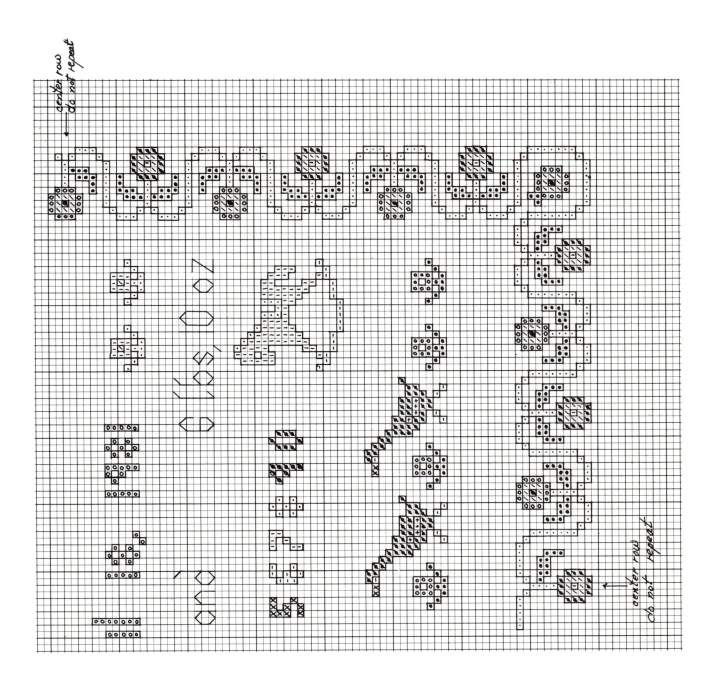

Lower Section

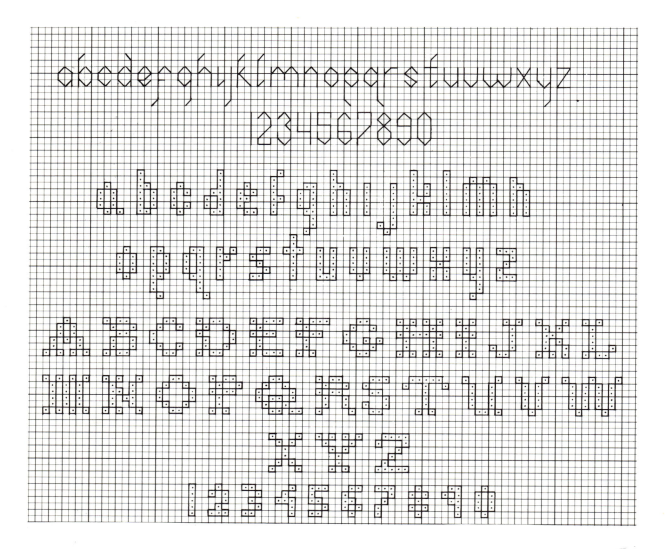

shown on the working chart are as follows: Lowercase alphabet: *a*, 350; *b*, 701; *c*, 826; *d*, 761; *e*, 741; *o*, 826; *p*, 761; *q*, 741; *r*, 975; *s*, 891. Numerals: *1*, 891; *2*, 701; *3*, 826; *4*, 761.

The little green motifs between the chicks are two Cross Stitches and a Straight Stitch at the top right to look like the illustration on the chart.

Remember when charting and working the piece that each square on the graph paper represents a stitch or a space two threads wide and two threads deep.

SCHOOLGIRL'S SAMPLER

Schoolgirls of the late eighteenth and early nineteenth centuries—particularly in the Northeast and in New England—learned discipline, symmetry, stitches and the rudiments of design on samplers not unlike this one. Some loved the work and designed beautiful pieces that are now prized as true examples of American folk art. The number of lovely samplers in both museum and private collections attests to the widespread use of the medium as a teaching tool.

The sampler is a particularly attractive decorative accent for a colonial home and makes a very personal and fitting gift for someone using eighteenth-century pieces in the home. This one looks unquestionably new because of its pure white background and pale colors. To add the look of age, use off-white Hardanger fabric and work in the deeper shades of color more often found in the old samplers.

This piece uses a quotation from the Bible—I John 3:12—a practice often found in the old samplers. You could use the space taken up by the Bible verse to change this to a wedding or birth record—or for any other occasion you might wish to mark, for that matter. Don't forget to work in your name and the date to help a museum date your work in the distant future!

center row
do not repeat

Top Section

center row
do not repeat

Middle heart-
shaped flower

center row
do not repeat

Lower Section   SCHOOLGIRL'S SAMPLER

⊙	472 Pale Green
·	471 Medium Green
•	470 Dark Green
╱	761 Pale Pink
✕	760 Medium Pink
◢	726 Pale Yellow
+	725 Gold
—	519 Pale Blue
‖	518 Medium Blue

COMPLETE ALPHABET AND QUOTATION FOR SCHOOLGIRL'S SAMPLER

FINISHED SIZE
15 × 20½ inches

MATERIALS

22-thread count white Hardanger fabric, at least 21 × 26½ inches

DMC cotton embroidery floss as follows: 472, Pale Green, 2 skeins; 471, Medium Green, 3 skeins; 470 Dark Green, 2 skeins; 761, Pale Pink, 2 skeins; 760, Medium Pink, 3 skeins; 726, Pale Yellow, 1 skein; 725, Gold, 1 skein; 519, Pale Blue, 1 skein; 518, Medium Blue, 1 skein

Mats and framing materials as shown (This custom-size frame was made at home following the suggestions and instructions on page 121.)

NOTE

Separate the embroidery floss and work all stitches with three strands.

Work all stitches over a square of four threads so the stitches count 11 to the inch.

INSTRUCTIONS

Cut the fabric and stitch along the edges to prevent fraying. With sewing thread place a basting thread through the vertical center row line as indicated on the chart. Also place a horizontal basting thread along the thread indicated at the center row of the middle heart-shaped flower on the side border. (This is not the horizontal center line, but the best reference point in the side border.)

For most people the best place to begin working is at the top center of the border, placing the tip of the heart-shaped flower on the center basting line about 3 inches down from the top edge of the fabric. From that point it is easy to count out the border and then begin working the interior patterns. Remember when counting mesh to place those interior designs so that each square on the graph represents a square of four threads.

Only the right half of the alphabet and the quotation are shown on the charts. These appear in entirety on page 148 and are keyed with the proper color codes to finish the sampler. Spacing is correct to fit into the design.

The vertical lines in the blue border at the top are simply Straight Stitches placed under the Cross Stitches. All other stitches are Cross Stitch placed as shown on the charts.

Block the finished embroidery. Mat and frame as shown.

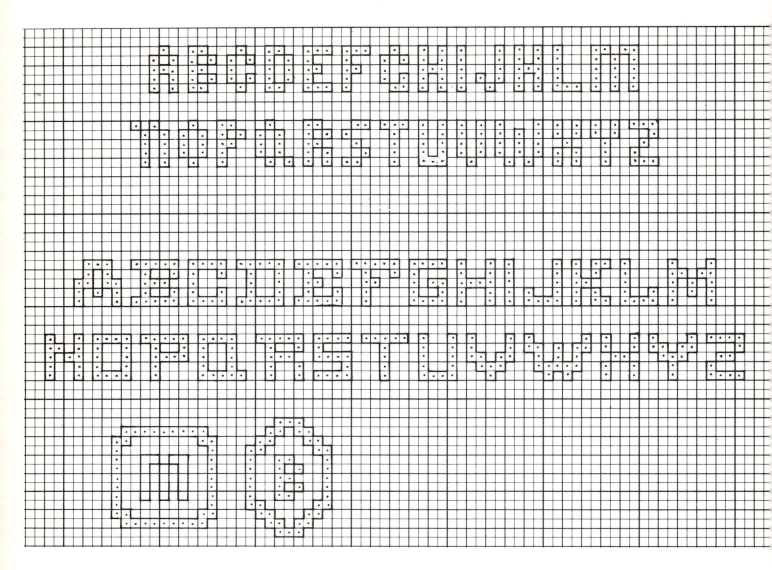

Alphabets

A gift of embroidery is more meaningful and has that extra personal touch if you sign it with your initials and the date of the occasion for which it was made. This assortment of small alphabets will help you plan your signature.

It is helpful to plan lettering on graph paper. If you are working with counted stitches, just choose the style and lay them out, spacing them as they appear on the chart.

Some alphabets include both capitals and lowercase letters, others just one. You may use all of one or the traditional combination. If you haven't done it before, you may want to develop your own little logo to use on all your projects. Consider a simple square, rectangle or diamond with your initial or initials centered inside. The ideas sketched illustrate how much the little frame adds. You can make the initial very prominent by working it in a color that contrasts with the back-ground area, or you can work in a color very close to the background and achieve a very subtle effect.

For embroidery on fabric it is very elegant to use your own signature, and this is actually very easy. Just write your name on a piece of tissue; then turn it over and go over it with a copy pencil to make a transfer pattern. Embroider with small stitches to preserve the curves—Whipped Back Stitch works very well.

If you can lay out the record information on pieces like the Pennsylvania Dutch Wedding Sampler in your own script, your work will be much enhanced. If you'd rather, use one of the script alphabets. Use a transparent graph paper; use one line as the base line; then trace the letters needed, spacing them as they are spaced on the charts. Several styles and sizes are included so you can use one that best fits your needs.

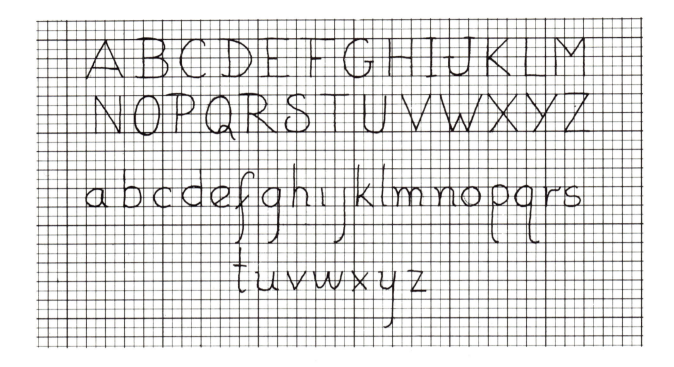

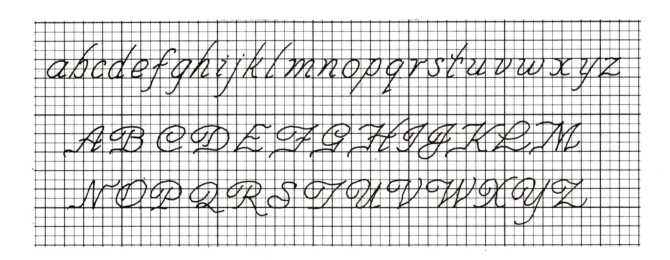

Finishing

At last, the embroidery is finished—it's a good feeling! The working was pleasurable, but the last moments putting in the final stitches and then admiring the completed piece are very special. Savor the feeling and look at the piece critically. This is the time when I sometimes find stitches that aren't perfect or even a whole section that doesn't satisfy me. This is the time to make corrections, and the few moments it takes are well spent.

There are several schools of thought about mistakes. Some believe that a few imperfections add to the charm, and in some cultures it is believed that only God can make something truly perfect so a few flaws are deliberately introduced. I have never accepted either theory, feeling that anything worth doing is worth the effort of doing it to the

best of one's ability. Also, I have noticed that if a mistake is left in a piece, the embroiderer is always conscious of it and hopes no one will notice. This greatly impairs the enjoyment of the finished embroidery and for me makes it imperative that flaws be repaired or removed. You'll be happier, too, knowing your work reflects the best in you.

BLOCKING

The next step is blocking and this too is of utmost importance. Blocking will smooth out stitches, restore texture, revive crushed fabric and make the piece look new. No matter how carefully the material has been handled during the embroidery process, it needs a final steaming or blocking before it is made up into the finished article. Soiled pieces may need washing, and wrinkled

153

pieces really need attention, but even the most disreputable will emerge from the blocking process looking fresh and new.

The equipment necessary for blocking embroidery is not expensive and is often already on hand. The list includes a blocking board, rustproof tacks or nails, T-square, hammer, and either a steam iron that produces a good jet of steam or one of the new little steaming devices designed for home sewers. These little steamers are wonders for they will not scorch fabric or flatten stitches, but they produce enough steam to even out stitches and dampen fabrics.

If you plan to do a lot of blocking, investigate the many new and simplified devices that have recently come on the market and have replaced the sheet of plywood as the favorite blocking base. Many are very easy to use and speed the process considerably. My favorite is a large sheet of pressed board which has been marked off into squares and circles and is perforated at 1-inch intervals with holes for nails. It comes with a good supply of rustproof nails, is well ventilated, easy to store and very easy to use. Another satisfactory type works much like the old-fashioned curtain stretcher. Check several shops or catalogs to see the various types and choose the one best for you. If you prefer your plywood, stick to it. The idea is to make the task fast and easy.

Embroidery on Fabric

If the embroidery is clean, fasten it dry to the blocking board with the stitches facing up. Pull the fabric taut and fasten it firmly. Steam thoroughly and allow it to dry on the board. If the steamer is not available, dampen the fabric evenly with an atomizer or sponge and leave it to dry.

Soiled embroidery should be washed carefully with cold water and mild soap. If you use one of the liquid detergents designed for fine fabrics, follow the directions and allow the piece to soak the prescribed number of minutes (but no longer), agitate gently to remove the soil, but do not rub. Do not ever just put the piece in the water and leave it for a good long soak. The colors may run and the soak is really not necessary. Try not to rub as this can mat yarns and disturb stitches. Rinse thoroughly—as many times as necessary until water is perfectly clear—because soap residue can be very damaging over a number of years.

Do not wring, but roll the piece in an absorbent towel and squeeze out excess moisture. Fasten the wet embroidery to the blocking board with the right side up. Pull the fabric taut and use the T-square to make sure it is straight. Allow the piece to dry. This is the best and most effective method of blocking, especially when the embroidery is heavily worked or has large textured stitches.

Although as a general rule it is best to avoid using the iron to block embroidery, some flat pieces can be successfully blocked with one. If the piece is soiled, wash it as explained. Roll the clean piece in a towel.

If the finished embroidery is clean, roll it in a wet towel and leave it until it is thoroughly and evenly moistened.

Pad the ironing table with a double thickness of heavy terry toweling and iron the wrong side of the embroidery piece until it is dry, pulling it as necessary to straighten. The heavy padding on the table will maintain the texture of the stitches. Be careful not to scorch the fabric and never touch the iron to the right side of the piece!

EMBROIDERY ON CANVAS

Since most needlepoint is badly out of shape, wet blocking is usually the best method of straightening the piece and smoothing the stitches. To wet the canvas and yarn evenly, roll the piece in a towel that has been wet in cold water and let it stand overnight. Fasten the dampened canvas to the blocking board, pulling as necessary to straighten, checking with the T-square and placing the rustproof tacks about 1 inch apart. Leave the canvas on the board to dry thoroughly. Drying times will vary, but the piece should not be removed until it is completely dry or it will revert to its unblocked shape.

Needlepoint that has been worked entirely in the Tent Stitch can be blocked with the right side to the board or with the right side facing up according to individual preference in the final appearance of the stitches. When blocked with the right side to the board, the stitches are slightly flattened and very smooth. Blocked face up, stitches are still smooth but have a more rounded appearance. If a piece contains a variety of crewel or textured needlepoint stitches, it should always be tacked to the board with the right side up to preserve the depth of the stitches. Bargello is prettier when the stitches retain their softness as when it is blocked with the right side facing up.

Since Bargello stitches do not pull the canvas out of shape, many completed pieces need only to be fastened to the blocking board and steamed. Again, the little triangular steamer is ideal, as it produces enough steam to loft the wool but will not scorch or flatten the stitches. The piece also dries very quickly after this treatment and will maintain its shape as well as a piece blocked by the conventional wet method. If you substitute the steam iron for the steamer, do not allow the iron to rest on the Bargello at any time.

Bargello that is badly misshapen and crumpled should be blocked wet. This method is usually best also for pieces that combine both Bargello and the Tent Stitch as the latter has a tendency to distort the canvas and produce a piece that needs a little more attention.

Occasionally it seems impossible to straighten a piece of needlepoint on the blocking board. This usually happens with a piece worked in the Continental Stitch. It can be trying. Pull and tack it as straight as possible and allow it to dry. Now, take it off the board, soak it again and start over. You will find that it will usually straighten out.

Good blocking is essential to good construction, for there is no way to sew a crooked piece of needlepoint into a square pillow and no way to make a lopsided picture look right in a frame.

CONSTRUCTION

PILLOWS

Pillows are the needleworker's favorite project, but many lament that the cost of having one assembled professionally is too expensive, and they are afraid to take a chance on trying to do the job themselves.

This is a shame for a pillow is a project that an average sewer can turn out in a very short time and one that can look very professional if only a little care goes into the sewing. Admittedly, the needlepoint is an expensive piece of fabric, but it is just that—a piece of fabric—and if you can make a pillow from another material, you can finish up your needlepoint or crewel, save some money, and still be proud of the finished pillow.

If you have never made a pillow, purchase an extra ½ yard of the backing that you choose and make up a companion pillow before working with the embroidery. This way you'll gain confidence and expertise—and you'll have an extra pillow.

The materials needed for making a pillow are: appropriate fabric for the back; cable cord (a soft white cotton cord from the drapery department); polyester fiber filling or a pillow form 1 inch larger than the finished pillow is to be in both length and width; and matching thread. Use the zipper or cording foot on the machine for professinal-looking results.

Trim the unworked borders of the blocked embroidery to ⅝ inch. Using the piece as a pattern, cut the fabric backing material to the same size. Cut a length of cable cord 1 inch longer than the total distance around the sides of the trimmed piece of embroidery. Cut a 1¼-inch-wide bias strip as long as the cable cord. Cut on the true bias, and piece the strip if necessary. Fold the bias strip in half lengthwise, insert the cord into the fold, and stitch as close to the cord as possible to make self-piping for insertion into the seams of the pillow.

With the embroidered pillow top right-side-up and beginning at the center of the bottom edge, pin the piping along the edge of the last row of stitches (if needlepoint or Bargello) or ⅝ inch from the cut edge of the fabric. Pin the cording with the cut edges along the raw edges of the fabric or canvas. Clip the cording at the corners so a sharp right-angle turn can be made. Overlap the ends of the piping and lead them toward the raw edges. Machine stitch the cording in place, stitching as close as possible to the cord.

Place the fabric for the back on a flat surface with the right side up. Position the embroidery on top with the wrong side up. Pin the layers together. Sew together, using the line of stitching holding the cording in place as a guide line. Leave the bottom partially open to receive the filling. Trim the seams and corners. Turn right side out. Fill with loose fiber filling or a purchased pillow form as you prefer. (The fiber filling will produce a softer pillow.) Slip-stitch to close the opening.

PINCUSHIONS
A sachet or pincushion is only a tiny pillow, and the basic construction is the same. Proceed as for a pillow and add lace, tassels, or other trimmings in the seam as desired. To use a sachet, fill with dried flowers or potpourri instead of fiber filling.

EYEGLASS CASE
For the lining of an eyeglass case choose a soft, lint-free fabric that will add a small amount of protection for the glasses as well as a touch of luxury. Velveteen and corduroy are good choices. When the embroidery is needlepoint, the canvas usually has enough body not to need an interfacing, but a cover of linen or other soft fabric will probably

need some inner support. You can choose one of the new ones that iron on or the conventional fabric types. Either is easy to handle.

Trim the unworked borders of the blocked embroidery to ½ inch on all sides. Using the trimmed piece as a pattern, cut the lining. With right sides together, fold the lining in half so it will correspond to the shape of the finished eyeglass case. Sew the bottom and side seams. Trim the seam allowance to ⅛ inch, but do not turn the lining.

With the steam iron, carefully press all seam allowances of the needlepoint or embroidery to the wrong side. If the piece is needlepoint, turn back part of the stitches of the last row so no canvas will be visible when the case is assembled.

With matching yarn or thread, beginning at the bottom edge and working from the right side, whip the case together as far as the corner. Insert the lining and continue joining to the top of the case. Turn to inside the seam allowance at the top of the lining and whip it to the edge of the case.

FRAMING

A discussion about framing of embroidery can easily lead to an argument or an attempt to establish inflexible rules about the proper use of glass and mats. Keep in mind the fact that there is usually more than one correct way to frame a given piece and that each individual piece should be considered in the light of personal preference as well as artistic value before any decision is made about framing materials. Styles in embroidery and home decoration vary so greatly that many finishing techniques need to be examined to be sure the correct look is achieved for each piece. While one piece may need a colored mat and classic frame, another may benefit from a wide ornate frame, and still another may be shown to greatest advantage in an elegant oval. One may look best stretched tightly against a flat surface, while another needs a soft padded look. The list could go on and on, but the essence is that the choice should be carefully considered and should complement—not overpower—the embroidery.

One of the biggest questions involves the use of glass over embroidery. In most instances it is best to frame without glass. While glass protects the embroidery from airborne dirt, it also obscures texture and may flatten stitches. Etched glareproof glass slightly darkens colors. Most dust can be easily and safely brushed from the surface of an embroidered picture, but in areas where there is extreme pollution there is just no alternative to the use of glass for protection. Even when glass is used, embroidery should be removed from the frame and washed every three to five years to prevent rot.

A mat usually adds much to any art work including embroidery. It can highlight a color in the picture or simply add to the overall dimensions, but it is often the final flourish a picture needs. New mats covered in textures simulating linen, burlap, silk and grass cloth are unusually attractive with needlework. Plain board mats can be made really elegant by covering them with fabric, while standard mat board available in art supply stores offers a range of colors to enhance most any color scheme.

Many professional framers will not mat an embroidered picture unless it is going to be covered with glass. This is because few pieces are worked on fabric cut large enough to allow it to be pulled to the back and laced over hardboard. Unless a piece is fastened this way it will eventually loosen and bubble out around the mat. Assembly at home makes certain that the piece is securely fastened and thus avoids this problem.

Frames in various sizes stocked in lumber, hardware, variety and art supply stores make it easy to find the right style for a piece that fits into the standard size ranges. Frame sections of metal or wood that snap together come in many lengths to solve some problems with irregular size, while prefinished moldings to be cut and assembled to custom measurements make it possible to frame pieces of any size. Styles run the gamut from simple narrow classics to wide heavily carved types.

Whichever combination is chosen, it can usually be assembled at home at considerable savings, and I recommend purchasing the few tools necessary for the job and plunging in. Do-it-yourself tools have improved greatly, and you can buy an excellent little miter box and saw made especially for cutting framing materials. The new instant-hold glues make assembly easy and new professional-type mat cutters make it possible to cut a perfect mat—even with a beveled edge if you wish.

In many cities a new kind of do-it-yourself framing store is springing up. These stock a wide selection of mats and framing materials, and they provide individual working spaces equipped with the best professional frame-making tools. Some will cut your mat, and in most the degree of help offered depends entirely upon how much the customer seeks. The savings here are not quite as great as if you did the job at home, but you have no outlay for tools, and those offered for use in the shops are generally better than you would buy for yourself.

Measure mats carefully and cut just as carefully, always using a new blade in your mat cutter or utility knife. Block the embroidery and center it on a heavy chipboard cut to frame size. Pull the edges to the back and lace into place with heavy thread. (If there is not enough fabric to allow it to be pulled back, add extensions of similar-weight fabric, keeping the seams as flat as possible.)

Lacing is the best and most permanent method of fastening embroidery in a frame, and it allows for removal later without damage to the fabric. Never glue a piece of embroidery to a backing board to keep it flat. Many glues will eventually discolor or rot fabric, and the piece usually cannot be removed for any reason.

Chipboard is gray and sometimes imparts a dingy look to loosely woven or light-colored fabrics. To avoid this, use a double-weight illustration board or foam-core art board as a substitute. If your piece is of heirloom quality, buy museum-approved, acid-free board to use as backing.

A soft padded look can be achieved by placing a layer of polyester quilt batting under the embroidery before lacing it in place. For this look, lace the piece in place with less tension so the padding is not crushed. This is a pretty effect for crewel pieces and was used for the Oval Miniatures on page 116.

Place the stretched embroidery and mat (if one is to be used) in the frame. Back with cardboard and fasten in place with small nails or glazier's points. Cut a piece of brown wrapping paper—a grocery bag will do—about ¼ inch less than the outside dimensions of the frame. Place the paper over the back of the framed picture. It should come almost to the outside edges of the frame. Glue the paper to the frame only. When the glue has dried, dampen the paper slightly, and it will shrink to the taut fit professional framers achieve. The paper is extra protection and makes a neat finish.

OTHER PROJECTS

Special projects that require finishing instructions have all the information needed included in the directions that accompany them.